CULTURE DRIVES STRATEGY

UNLOCKING SUCCESS THROUGH ALIGNMENT

Why a Conducive Business Culture is Important for Executing Strategy

Dr. Pratik P. SURANA (Ph.D.)

INDIA • SINGAPORE • MALAYSIA

ISBN

Hardcase 979-8-89610-306-6
Paperback 979-8-89588-689-2

“For the timeless inspiration who inspires me in everything I do”

I dedicate this book to my late father Shri Prakashchandra SURANA, My mother Pushpa P SURANA, My parents Bai and Babuji, My Sister Pragati, My wife Anshima, My kids, Krisha and Meghav, My friends, Megha, Deepak, Mark, Anna, My Ate Vida ,Sunil and many more who understood each of my emotions. Least to say my colleagues at Quantum who understood each of my emotions and ensured we grew together.

Contents

Contents

Introduction

In the evolving landscape of modern business, strategy often takes center stage. Companies invest substantial resources in developing robust strategies that promise growth, innovation, and competitive edge. Yet, despite the meticulous planning and well-crafted roadmaps, many organizations struggle to realize their strategic objectives. The missing link frequently lies not in the strategy itself but in the business culture that surrounds it.

Business culture, the set of shared values, beliefs, and practices within an organization, plays a pivotal role in shaping how strategies are executed. It is the invisible hand that guides employee behavior, decision-making processes, and overall organizational dynamics. Without a conducive culture, even the most brilliant strategies can falter, stymied by resistance, misalignment, and lack of engagement.

This book delves into the critical importance of fostering a business culture that supports and enhances strategy execution. Through a blend of theoretical insights and practical examples, it explores how culture influences every facet of an organization, from leadership and communication to innovation and customer relations. It also provides actionable frameworks and tools for leaders to cultivate an environment where strategic initiatives can thrive.

Understanding the interplay between culture and strategy execution is not merely an academic exercise; it is a practical necessity for any organization aiming to achieve sustainable success. By harnessing the power of a conducive business culture, companies can unlock new levels of performance, agility, and resilience. This book aims to illuminate this often-overlooked aspect of strategic management, offering readers the knowledge and tools to align their organizational culture with their strategic aspirations.

Chapter 01

Introduction to Business Culture and Strategy Execution

Defining Business Culture

Business culture is the invisible yet palpable force that drives the behavior, attitudes, and performance of an organization. It encompasses the values, beliefs, and norms shared by members of the organization, shaping how work gets done and how employees interact with each other and with external stakeholders. This culture is not merely a backdrop; it is a dynamic entity that evolves with the organization, influenced by leadership, policies, and the external environment.

At its core, business culture can be seen as the collective personality of an organization. It manifests in various ways, from the decision-making processes to the way conflicts are resolved. In many cases, it can be observed in the everyday rituals and routines, the stories and legends that circulate within the company, and the symbols and language used by its members. These elements combine to create a unique environment that can either propel an organization towards its strategic goals or hinder its progress.

Understanding business culture requires an appreciation of both its tangible and intangible elements. Tangible elements include formal policies, codes of conduct, and organizational structures. These are the visible aspects of culture that can be documented and analyzed. Intangible elements, on the other hand, are more abstract and include the unwritten rules and social norms that guide behavior. These are often more challenging to identify and change but are crucial in shaping the overall culture.

Leadership plays a pivotal role in defining and nurturing business culture. Leaders set the tone for the organization, modeling the behaviors and attitudes they wish to see in their employees. Through their actions and decisions, they communicate what is valued and what is not, influencing the culture in profound ways. Effective leaders are those who recognize the importance of culture and actively work to align it with the organization's strategic objectives.

Communication is another critical component in the development of business culture. Open and transparent communication fosters trust and collaboration, creating a sense of community and shared purpose. Conversely, a lack of communication can lead to misunderstandings, mistrust, and a fragmented culture. Organizations that prioritize effective communication are better positioned to execute their strategies successfully.

The external environment also plays a significant role in shaping business culture. Market conditions, industry trends, and regulatory landscapes can all influence how an organization operates and what it values. For instance, a company in a highly regulated industry may emphasize compliance and risk management, while a tech startup might prioritize innovation and agility. Understanding these external factors is essential for developing a culture that supports the organization's strategic goals.

Business culture is not static; it evolves over time as the organization grows and changes. Mergers, acquisitions, and leadership transitions can all have a profound impact on culture, necessitating deliberate efforts to manage and adapt it. Organizations that succeed in maintaining a strong, cohesive culture are those that continuously assess and refine their cultural elements, ensuring alignment with their strategic objectives.

In essence, business culture is the lifeblood of an organization, influencing every aspect of its operations. It is a powerful tool for strategy execution, providing the foundation upon which successful initiatives are built. By understanding and actively managing their culture, organizations can create an environment that supports their strategic goals and drives long-term success.

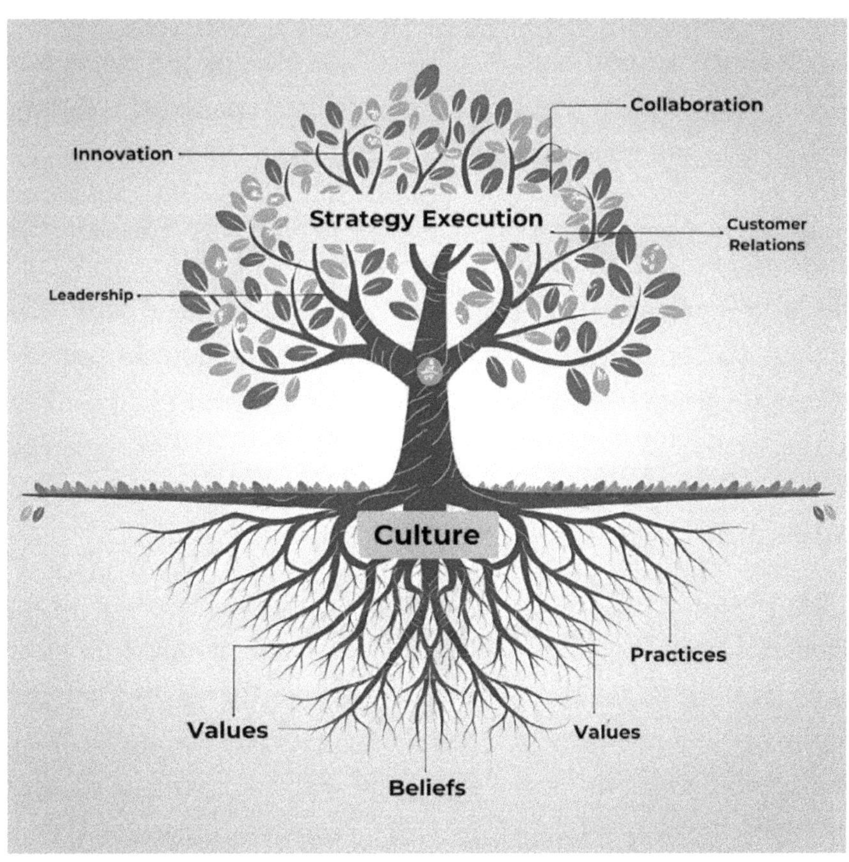

Understanding Strategy Execution

Strategy execution is a multifaceted process that involves translating strategic plans into actionable steps to achieve desired outcomes. It is where the grand vision and carefully crafted strategies meet the practical realities of day-to-day operations. Understanding strategy execution requires a deep dive into the mechanisms, behaviors, and cultural aspects that drive or hinder progress.

The foundation of effective strategy execution lies in aligning organizational resources, capabilities, and behaviors with the strategic objectives. This alignment involves ensuring that every department, team, and individual understands their role in the broader strategic context. It requires clear communication of the strategic goals and the specific contributions expected from each part of the organization. Without this clarity, efforts can become fragmented, leading to inefficiencies and missed targets.

Another critical component is the establishment of a robust framework for monitoring and evaluation. This framework should include key performance indicators (KPIs) that are closely tied to strategic objectives. Regular tracking of these KPIs allows organizations to measure progress, identify deviations from the plan, and make necessary adjustments. It also provides a basis for accountability, ensuring that individuals and teams are held responsible for their contributions to strategic goals.

Leadership plays a pivotal role in strategy execution. Effective leaders not only articulate the vision and strategic direction but also inspire and motivate their teams to achieve the desired outcomes. They create an environment where employees feel empowered to take initiative and make decisions that align with the strategic objectives. Leadership involvement also includes removing obstacles that may impede progress and providing the necessary resources and support to drive execution.

The organizational culture significantly influences strategy execution. A culture that fosters collaboration, innovation, and adaptability can enhance the execution process. Conversely, a culture resistant to change or characterized by silos can be a major barrier. Cultivating a culture that supports strategy execution involves promoting behaviors and mindsets that align with the strategic goals. This may include encouraging open communication, rewarding risk-taking and innovation, and fostering a sense of shared purpose and commitment.

Employee engagement is another crucial element. When employees are engaged, they are more likely to be committed to the organization's strategic goals and put in the effort required to achieve them. Engaged employees understand how their work contributes to the larger objectives and feel a sense of ownership and pride in their contributions. Organizations can enhance engagement through recognition programs, opportunities for professional growth, and creating a work environment that values and respects individual contributions.

Resource allocation is also a key factor in strategy execution. This involves ensuring that financial, human, and technological resources are appropriately distributed to support strategic initiatives. Effective resource allocation requires a thorough understanding of the priorities and potential impact of various initiatives. It also involves making tough decisions about where to allocate resources to maximize strategic outcomes.

Lastly, agility and flexibility are essential for successful strategy execution. The business environment is constantly changing, and organizations must be able to adapt their strategies and execution plans in response to new information and shifting conditions. This requires a willingness to experiment, learn from failures, and continuously refine approaches to stay aligned with strategic objectives.

Understanding strategy execution involves recognizing the interplay between clear communication, leadership, culture, engagement, resource allocation, and adaptability. By focusing on these elements, organizations can bridge the gap between strategic planning and operational success, ultimately achieving their desired outcomes.

The Interconnection between Culture and Strategy

Culture and strategy are two sides of the same coin in the realm of business execution. The former provides the context and environment in which the latter is formulated and implemented. A company's culture can be likened to the soil in which strategic plans are planted. Just as the quality of the soil affects the growth of a plant, the prevailing culture in an organization influences the success or failure of its strategic initiatives.

In organizations where culture and strategy are tightly interwoven, employees tend to exhibit higher levels of engagement and commitment. They understand the strategic objectives and feel a sense of ownership over the outcomes. This alignment fosters a collaborative atmosphere where everyone works towards common goals. When strategy is divorced from culture, however, dissonance arises, leading to inefficiencies and morale issues.

Consider the role of leadership in this dynamic. Leaders serve as the bridge between culture and strategy. Their actions and attitudes set the tone for the organizational culture, which in turn shapes how strategies are perceived and executed by the workforce. Leaders who are mindful of this interconnection often invest time and resources in cultivating a culture that supports strategic objectives. This might involve fostering open communication, encouraging risk-taking, and rewarding innovation.

Communication is another crucial element that ties culture and strategy together. A transparent and open communication culture ensures that employees at all levels are aware of the strategic goals and understand their role in achieving them. Regular updates, feedback loops, and inclusive discussions help in demystifying the strategy and making it accessible. When employees are kept in the loop, they are more likely to align their actions with the strategic direction of the company.

Moreover, the values and beliefs inherent in an organization's culture can act as a compass for strategic decisions. For instance, a company that values sustainability will naturally gravitate towards strategies that promote environmental responsibility. In this way, culture not only shapes the execution of existing strategies but also informs the development of new ones. It provides a framework within which strategic choices are made, ensuring consistency and coherence in decision-making.

Employee behavior is also a manifestation of the interplay between culture and strategy. In a culture that prioritizes customer satisfaction, employees will intuitively align their actions to enhance the customer experience, thereby supporting the company's strategic focus on customer-centricity. Conversely, in a culture that is hierarchical and risk-averse, employees may hesitate to take the initiative, which can stifle innovation and hinder strategic progress.

The physical and virtual environments of a workplace can also reflect and reinforce the cultural and strategic alignment. Open-plan offices, flexible working hours, and collaborative tools can signify a culture that values openness, flexibility, and teamwork, which are essential for executing strategies that require cross-functional collaboration and agility.

The recruitment and onboarding process is another touchpoint where culture and strategy intersect. Hiring individuals who not only possess the necessary skills but also fit the cultural mold of the organization ensures that new hires are predisposed to support and advance strategic objectives. A well-thought-out onboarding process can further inculcate the strategic vision and cultural norms, setting the stage for long-term alignment.

The relationship between culture and strategy is symbiotic. Culture provides the fertile ground for strategy to take root, grow, and flourish. In turn, a well-executed strategy reinforces and strengthens the culture, creating a virtuous cycle that propels the organization forward. Understanding and leveraging this interconnection is crucial for any business aiming for sustainable success.

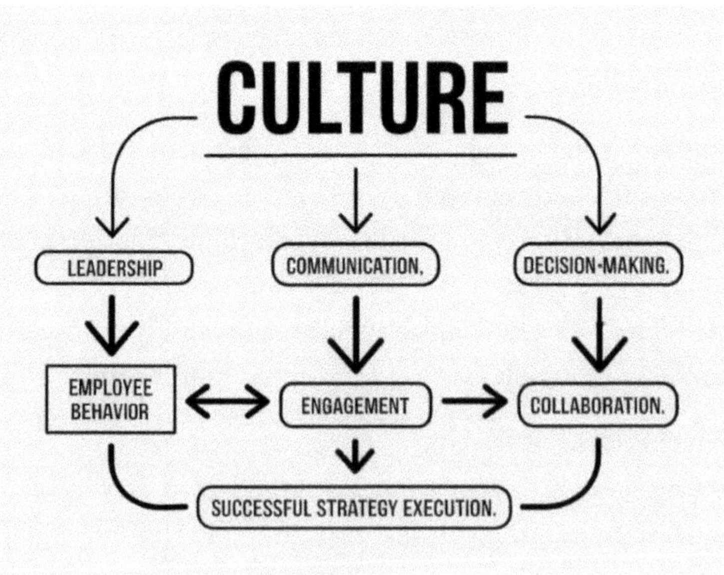

Importance of Aligning Culture with Strategy

In the dynamic landscape of modern business, the interplay between organizational culture and strategic execution cannot be overstated. Organizational culture, the collective values, beliefs, and behaviors that shape how work gets done, serves as the bedrock upon which strategic initiatives are built. When culture and strategy are in harmony, companies find themselves in a position where they can execute their plans more effectively, respond to market changes swiftly, and achieve their goals with greater precision.

A misalignment between culture and strategy often leads to friction. Employees may struggle to adapt to new strategic directions if they conflict with the ingrained cultural norms. For instance, a company that values stability and risk-aversion may find it challenging to shift towards an innovation-driven strategy. The employees, accustomed to a cautious approach, may resist the push for rapid experimentation and change, thereby stalling strategic initiatives. This resistance is not born from a lack of capability but from a misalignment of underlying values.

Conversely, when culture supports the strategy, the entire organization moves in unison towards common objectives. Imagine a technology firm aiming to become a leader in cutting-edge innovations. If the company's culture promotes creativity, encourages risk-taking, and rewards novel ideas, the strategy of leading through innovation is naturally supported by the day-to-day behaviors of its employees. This cultural alignment ensures that initiatives aimed at fostering innovation are met with enthusiasm rather than resistance.

Moreover, aligning culture with strategy enhances internal coherence and consistency. When the cultural values resonate with strategic goals, decision-making processes become more streamlined. Employees at all levels understand the strategic priorities and can make decisions that are congruent with the overarching objectives. This coherence reduces ambiguity and fosters a sense of purpose across the organization. It also mitigates the risk of conflicting priorities that can arise when cultural values and strategic goals are at odds.

Leadership plays a pivotal role in aligning culture with strategy. Leaders must embody the cultural values that support the strategic direction of the company. Their actions, decisions, and communication set the tone for the rest of the organization. When leaders consistently demonstrate a commitment to the cultural values that underpin the strategy, they reinforce the desired behaviors and attitudes among employees. This alignment between leadership behavior and strategic goals creates a powerful synergy that propels the organization forward.

Additionally, aligning culture with strategy can significantly enhance employee engagement and morale. When employees see a clear connection between their work, the cultural values they believe in, and the strategic goals of the organization, their sense of belonging and purpose is strengthened. This alignment fosters a positive work environment where employees are motivated to contribute to the company's success. High levels of engagement translate into increased productivity, lower turnover rates, and a stronger competitive edge.

In the realm of strategic execution, the alignment of culture and strategy acts as a catalyst for success. It creates a cohesive environment where strategic initiatives are supported by the collective behaviors and attitudes of the workforce. This alignment not only facilitates smoother implementation of strategic plans but also builds a resilient organization capable of navigating the complexities of the business world. By recognizing the importance of this alignment, companies can harness the full potential of their cultural strengths to achieve their strategic aspirations.

Chapter 02

The Role of Leadership in Shaping Business Culture

Leadership Styles and Organizational Culture

Leadership styles and organizational culture are fundamentally intertwined, each influencing and shaping the other in a continuous loop of interaction. Leadership style refers to the manner and approach of providing direction, implementing plans, and motivating people. It is the way in which leaders convey their vision, values, and expectations to their team members. Organizational culture, on the other hand, is the collective behavior of individuals within an organization, encompassing the shared values, beliefs, and norms that influence how employees interact with one another and approach their work.

Different leadership styles can significantly impact the culture of an organization. For instance, an autocratic leadership style, characterized by individual control over all decisions and little input from group members, tends to create a culture of dependency and limited innovation. Employees in such environments may feel less empowered to take initiative or suggest new ideas, leading to a more rigid and less adaptive organizational culture.

Conversely, a democratic leadership style, which involves participative decision-making and encourages input from team members, fosters a culture of collaboration and inclusivity. In such an environment, employees are more likely to feel valued and engaged, contributing to a dynamic and innovative organizational culture. This style promotes open communication, trust, and mutual respect, which can enhance team morale and productivity.

Transformational leadership, which inspires and motivates employees to exceed their own self-interests for the good of the organization, is known to cultivate a culture of high performance and continuous improvement. Transformational leaders lead by example, setting high standards and encouraging their team members to strive for excellence. This style can instill a sense of purpose and drive within the organization, leading to a culture that embraces change and values personal and professional growth.

On the other hand, transactional leadership, which focuses on routine, supervision, and performance-related rewards and punishments, tends to create a more structured and stable organizational culture. While this style can be effective in achieving short-term goals and maintaining order, it may not foster the same level of innovation and employee engagement as other styles. Employees in such environments may feel motivated primarily by extrinsic rewards, which can limit their intrinsic motivation and creativity.

The alignment between leadership style and organizational culture is crucial for the successful execution of business strategies. Leaders must be aware of the existing culture within their organization and consider how their leadership style will either reinforce or transform that culture. For example, a leader aiming to implement a strategy that requires high levels of innovation and adaptability must adopt a leadership style that encourages these attributes, such as transformational or democratic leadership.

In contrast, if a strategy requires strict adherence to processes and consistency, a more transactional or autocratic leadership style may be appropriate. However, leaders must also be mindful of the potential downsides of each style and strive to balance their approach to suit the specific needs and context of their organization.

Understanding the interplay between leadership styles and organizational culture is vital for leaders seeking to effectively execute their business strategies. By consciously aligning their leadership approach with the desired cultural attributes, leaders can create an environment that supports and enhances strategic objectives, ultimately driving organizational success.

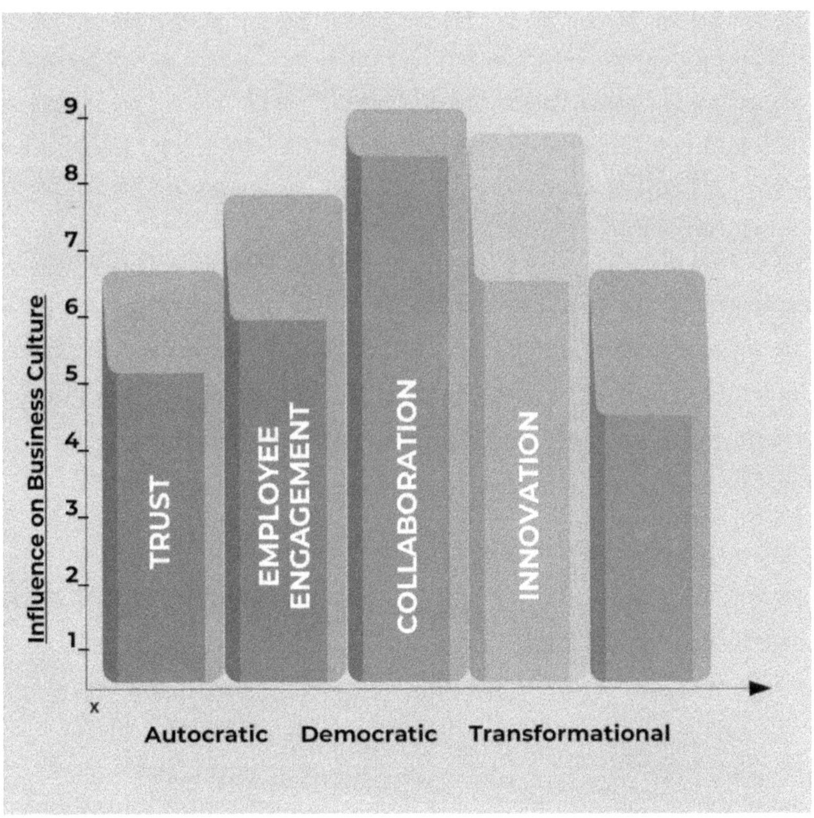

Creating a Vision for Culture

A thriving business culture is not an accidental occurrence but a carefully crafted vision that aligns seamlessly with a company's strategic goals. This vision serves as the foundation upon which the edifice of a strong organizational culture is built. The process of creating a vision for culture begins with a deep understanding of the organization's core values, mission, and long-term objectives. These elements must resonate with every member of the organization, from the top executives to the newest recruits.

Imagine an intricate tapestry, where each thread represents a different aspect of the company's ethos. These threads need to be woven together with precision and intention to create a coherent and compelling picture. This picture, or vision, should encapsulate what the organization stands for and where it aspires to go. It should be aspirational yet achievable, providing a clear direction while allowing room for individual and collective growth.

A critical step in this process is engaging all stakeholders in the dialogue about culture. Leaders must solicit input from various levels within the organization to ensure that the vision is inclusive and reflective of the diverse perspectives that make up the company. This collective input not only enriches the vision but also fosters a sense of ownership and commitment among employees.

Once a preliminary vision is articulated, it must be communicated effectively throughout the organization. This communication should be continuous and multifaceted, utilizing various channels to reach different audiences. Town hall meetings, internal newsletters, and digital platforms can be leveraged to share the vision and its significance. The message must be consistent and reinforced regularly to ensure it permeates every layer of the organization.

It is equally important to align the vision with the company's strategic initiatives. The vision for culture should not be an abstract concept but a tangible framework that guides decision-making, behaviors, and practices. For instance, if innovation is a cornerstone of the vision, then strategies should be in place to encourage creative thinking and risk-taking. This alignment ensures that the culture supports and enhances the company's strategic objectives rather than hindering them.

Metrics and feedback mechanisms are essential in this phase to evaluate the effectiveness of the vision. Regular surveys, focus groups, and performance reviews can provide insights into how well the vision is being integrated into daily operations. These tools help identify gaps and areas for improvement, allowing leaders to make necessary adjustments.

Leaders play a pivotal role in embodying and championing the vision. Their actions and decisions should consistently reflect the cultural aspirations of the organization. By modeling the desired behaviors and attitudes, leaders set a powerful example for others to follow. This top-down approach ensures that the vision is not just a statement on paper but a living, breathing part of the organizational fabric.

Recognition and rewards systems can also reinforce the vision. Acknowledging and celebrating individuals and teams who exemplify the cultural values helps to embed the vision into the organizational psyche. This positive reinforcement encourages others to align their actions with the cultural vision.

Creating a vision for culture is an ongoing process that requires dedication, transparency, and adaptability. As the organization evolves, so too should the vision, ensuring it remains relevant and inspiring. This dynamic approach not only sustains the culture but also propels the organization toward its strategic goals with a unified and motivated workforce.

Leaders as Cultural Champions

Leaders wield unparalleled influence within an organization, acting as the linchpin between strategic vision and operational execution. Their role transcends mere management; they shape, nurture, and embody the very essence of the company's culture. The essence of a robust business culture lies in its ability to translate strategic objectives into actionable practices, a feat achieved only when leaders are not just administrators but champions of culture.

Effective leaders understand that culture is not a static entity but a dynamic force that evolves with the organization. They are astute observers of their environment, perceptive to the subtle shifts in employee behavior, and responsive to the changing needs of the market. These leaders recognize that the alignment of culture with strategy is not incidental but intentional, requiring deliberate actions and consistent reinforcement.

The most impactful leaders are those who lead by example. Their actions, decisions, and interactions serve as a model for the entire organization. When leaders consistently demonstrate the values and behaviors they wish to see in their teams, they create a powerful ripple effect. Employees, inspired by their leaders, are more likely to adopt and internalize these cultural norms, fostering a cohesive and unified organizational ethos.

Communication is a pivotal tool in a leader's arsenal. Transparent, frequent, and authentic communication helps to articulate the organization's vision and values clearly. Leaders who communicate effectively ensure that every member of the organization understands their role in the larger strategic framework. This clarity not only motivates employees but also aligns their efforts with the company's long-term goals.

Moreover, leaders play a critical role in recognizing and rewarding behaviors that align with the desired culture. By celebrating successes and acknowledging contributions that reinforce the company's values, leaders reinforce the importance of cultural alignment. These positive reinforcements serve as tangible reminders of what the organization stands for, further embedding these values into the daily operations of the business.

In times of change or crisis, the true test of a leader's commitment to culture becomes evident. Leaders who prioritize cultural integrity during challenging periods demonstrate resilience and steadfastness. Their ability to navigate turbulence while upholding the organization's core values provides a stabilizing force, ensuring that the company remains anchored to its foundational principles.

Furthermore, the development of future leaders within the organization is a testament to a leader's role as a cultural champion. By mentoring and cultivating emerging talent, current leaders ensure the perpetuation of the organization's culture. This succession planning is crucial for the sustainability of the company's values and strategic vision.

Leaders who are cultural champions understand that their influence extends beyond the immediate confines of their organization. They are often seen as representatives of the company's brand and reputation in the broader market. Their commitment to culture can enhance the organization's standing with customers, partners, and other stakeholders, creating a positive external perception that can drive business success.

In essence, leaders as cultural champions are the custodians of their organization's ethos. Their ability to embody, communicate, and reinforce the company's values is integral to the successful execution of strategy. By fostering a culture that aligns with strategic objectives, they ensure that the organization not only survives but thrives in a competitive landscape. Their leadership is a beacon, guiding the organization towards sustained excellence and growth.

Case Studies of Effective Leadership

In the intricate dance of strategy execution within the realm of business culture, effective leadership stands as the cornerstone. The following case studies exemplify how distinct leadership styles and decisions can significantly influence organizational outcomes.

Consider the case of a multinational technology firm navigating a period of rapid expansion. The CEO, renowned for his visionary leadership, spearheaded a transformative strategy to penetrate emerging markets. His approach was characterized by a deep commitment to cultural intelligence. By immersing himself in the local cultures of target markets, he gained invaluable insights that informed the company's strategy. This cultural sensitivity was reflected in tailored marketing campaigns, localized product features, and strategic partnerships with local businesses. The CEO's ability to meld global strategy with local nuances not only bolstered market penetration but also fostered a sense of respect and trust among new customer bases. This case underscores the pivotal role of culturally attuned leadership in executing strategies that resonate on a global scale.

In another instance, a leading financial services company faced the challenge of digital transformation. The COO, known for her collaborative leadership style, orchestrated a cross-functional task force to drive the initiative. She fostered an environment where diverse perspectives were not only welcomed but actively sought. By leveraging the collective expertise of IT, marketing, and customer service teams, the company developed a comprehensive digital strategy that addressed both internal efficiencies and customer experiences. The COO's emphasis on collaboration and inclusivity ensured that the transformation was holistic, encompassing technological upgrades, process innovations, and cultural shifts. Her leadership exemplified how fostering a culture of collaboration and inclusivity can be instrumental in executing complex, multi-faceted strategies.

A different scenario unfolded within a traditional manufacturing company aiming to adopt sustainable practices. The company's president, a staunch advocate for sustainability, led by example. He initiated a company-wide sustainability program that included reducing waste, optimizing energy use, and sourcing eco-friendly materials. His transparent communication about the environmental and economic benefits of these practices garnered widespread support from employees at all levels. By aligning the company's strategic goals with broader environmental values, he not only enhanced the company's reputation but also achieved substantial cost savings. This case highlights how values-driven leadership can align organizational strategy with ethical imperatives, driving both business success and social responsibility.

Lastly, a prominent retail chain faced dwindling market share due to increasing competition. The newly appointed CEO, recognized for her adaptive leadership, implemented a turnaround strategy focused on innovation and customer engagement. She encouraged a culture of experimentation, where employees were empowered to test new ideas and approaches. Under her leadership, the company launched several innovative initiatives, including a revamped loyalty program and an enhanced online shopping experience. The CEO's adaptive approach allowed the company to swiftly respond to market changes and customer preferences, ultimately revitalizing its market position. This example illustrates how adaptive leadership can foster a culture of innovation and agility, crucial for navigating competitive landscapes.

These case studies demonstrate the multifaceted nature of effective leadership in strategy execution. Whether through cultural intelligence, collaboration, values-driven initiatives, or adaptive strategies, these leaders exemplified how aligning leadership styles with organizational culture can drive successful strategy execution. Their stories provide valuable insights into the diverse ways leadership can shape and steer the course of business strategy in an ever-evolving landscape.

Chapter 03

Assessing and Diagnosing Your Current Culture

Tools for Cultural Assessment

Understanding the cultural nuances within an organization is crucial for the seamless execution of any strategic plan. In a world where businesses are increasingly operating in diverse and multicultural environments, the need to assess and comprehend cultural dynamics cannot be overstated. The tools for cultural assessment offer a structured approach to uncovering the underlying beliefs, values, and behaviors that drive an organization.

One of the primary tools used in cultural assessment is the Organizational Culture Assessment Instrument (OCAI). Developed by Kim Cameron and Robert Quinn, this tool is based on the Competing Values Framework. It allows organizations to identify their dominant culture type by evaluating six key dimensions: dominant characteristics, organizational leadership, management of employees, organizational glue, strategic emphases, and criteria of success. By plotting these dimensions on a grid, businesses can visualize their cultural profile and identify areas that may need alignment with strategic objectives.

Another valuable tool is the Cultural Web, introduced by Gerry Johnson and Kevan Scholes. This framework helps organizations map out the elements that constitute their culture, including stories, rituals, symbols, power structures, organizational structures, control systems, and paradigms. By examining these components, businesses gain insights into the cultural forces at play and how they impact strategic initiatives. The Cultural Web is particularly useful for identifying cultural strengths and weaknesses, providing a comprehensive picture of the organizational environment.

Surveys and questionnaires are also widely used in cultural assessments. These tools gather quantitative data on employees' perceptions and attitudes towards various cultural aspects. The Denison Organizational Culture Survey, for instance, measures cultural traits such as involvement, consistency, adaptability, and mission. By analyzing survey results, organizations can pinpoint cultural attributes that support or hinder strategic goals, allowing for targeted interventions.

Focus groups and interviews offer a qualitative approach to cultural assessment. These methods involve engaging with employees at different levels to gain deeper insights into their experiences and perspectives. Through open-ended discussions, organizations can uncover implicit cultural norms and values that may not be evident through quantitative measures. Focus groups and interviews provide rich, contextual data that can be invaluable for understanding the subtleties of organizational culture.

Ethnographic studies represent another powerful tool for cultural assessment. This method involves immersing oneself in the organizational environment to observe and document cultural practices firsthand. Ethnographers take on the role of participant-observers, engaging with employees in their daily activities to gain a nuanced understanding of the culture. While time-consuming, ethnographic studies offer a detailed, ground-level view of the cultural landscape, making them particularly effective for capturing the complexities of organizational life.

Combining multiple assessment tools can yield a more comprehensive understanding of organizational culture. For example, using surveys to gather broad quantitative data, followed by focus groups to explore specific areas in detail, can provide a balanced view. This multi-method approach ensures that both the measurable and intangible aspects of culture are considered, leading to more informed strategic decisions.

The choice of assessment tools should be guided by the specific needs and context of the organization. Whether through structured instruments, qualitative methods, or immersive studies, the goal is to uncover the cultural elements that influence strategic execution. By leveraging these tools effectively, businesses can align their cultural dynamics with their strategic objectives, paving the way for successful strategy implementation.

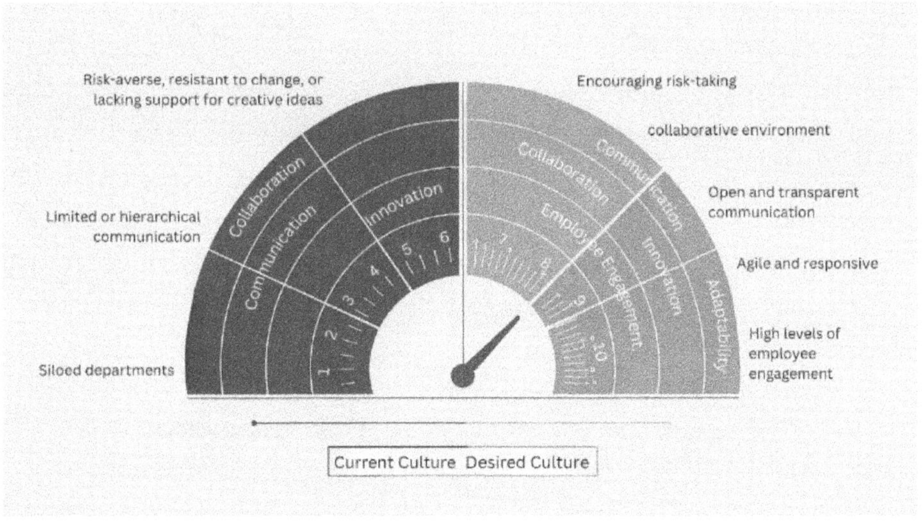

Identifying Cultural Strengths and Weaknesses

Understanding the intricacies of a company's culture is crucial for effective strategy execution. The ability to identify cultural strengths and weaknesses can determine the success or failure of strategic initiatives. A well-rounded comprehension of these cultural elements begins with a thorough analysis of the organization's core values, beliefs, and behaviors.

Core values are the fundamental principles that guide an organization's actions and decision-making processes. These values are often deeply ingrained and can be a source of strength when they align well with the company's strategic goals. For instance, a culture that values innovation will likely support strategies aimed at fostering creativity and new product development. On the other hand, if the core values are misaligned with the strategic objectives, they can become significant obstacles. An organization that prioritizes stability and risk aversion may struggle to implement strategies requiring rapid change or bold experimentation.

Beliefs within an organization shape how employees perceive their roles and the company's mission. These beliefs can either bolster or undermine strategic efforts. For example, if employees believe that their contributions are vital to the company's success, they are more likely to be engaged and proactive in executing the strategy. Conversely, if there is a pervasive belief that strategic initiatives are merely top-down mandates with little relevance to day-to-day operations, employee buy-in may be minimal, leading to poor execution.

Behaviors are the observable actions and interactions within the organization. These can provide clear indicators of cultural strengths and weaknesses. Positive behaviors, such as open communication, collaboration, and a willingness to take calculated risks, can enhance strategy execution. Negative behaviors, such as siloes thinking, resistance to change, and lack of accountability, can hinder progress and lead to strategic failures.

To identify these cultural elements, organizations can employ various diagnostic tools and methods. Surveys and questionnaires can capture employees' perceptions and attitudes, offering insights into the prevailing cultural norms. Focus groups and interviews provide a more nuanced understanding of the underlying beliefs and values that drive behaviors. Observational methods, such as ethnographic studies, can reveal how culture manifests in everyday work practices.

Once cultural strengths and weaknesses are identified, the next step is to leverage the strengths and address the weaknesses. Leveraging strengths involves building on the positive aspects of the culture that support strategic objectives. For example, if a company has a strong culture of teamwork, this can be harnessed to foster cross-functional collaboration on strategic projects. Addressing weaknesses requires targeted interventions to shift detrimental cultural elements. This might involve leadership development programs to instill new values, communication campaigns to reshape beliefs, or changes in policies and procedures to modify behaviors.

It is also essential to recognize that cultural change is a gradual process. Attempting to overhaul an organization's culture overnight is likely to meet with resistance and fail. A more effective approach is to implement incremental changes that align with the strategic goals while respecting the existing cultural context. Engaging employees at all levels in the change process can facilitate smoother transitions and ensure that the new cultural elements are embraced and sustained.

By systematically identifying and addressing cultural strengths and weaknesses, organizations can create a supportive environment for strategy execution. This alignment between culture and strategy not only enhances the likelihood of achieving strategic goals but also fosters a cohesive and motivated workforce, ultimately driving long-term success.

Stakeholder Perspectives

Stakeholders play a pivotal role in shaping and influencing the cultural dynamics that drive strategy execution within any organization. Their perspectives, expectations, and interactions can significantly impact the effectiveness of strategic initiatives. Understanding these diverse viewpoints is crucial for creating a cohesive and supportive business culture.

Employees, often regarded as the backbone of any organization, are primary stakeholders whose engagement and motivation directly affect strategy execution. They seek clarity in their roles, transparent communication, and recognition for their contributions. A culture that fosters trust, collaboration, and continuous learning can empower employees to align their efforts with the strategic goals of the organization. When employees feel valued and understand how their work contributes to the larger objectives, they are more likely to be committed and proactive in their roles.

Customers, another critical group of stakeholders, have expectations that extend beyond the products or services they purchase. They look for consistency, quality, and a positive experience in every interaction with the organization. A customer-centric culture that prioritizes understanding and meeting customer needs can enhance satisfaction and loyalty. Organizations that actively listen to customer feedback and adapt their strategies accordingly can build stronger relationships and drive long-term success.

Investors and shareholders, whose primary concern is the financial performance and growth of the organization, are also key stakeholders. They seek assurance that the strategic direction will yield profitable returns. A culture of accountability, innovation, and prudent risk management can instill confidence in investors. Transparent reporting and effective governance practices are essential to maintaining their trust and support. When investors perceive that the organizational culture aligns with sustainable growth and ethical practices, they are more likely to continue their investment and support strategic initiatives.

Suppliers and partners, who play a crucial role in the supply chain and operational efficiency, have their own set of expectations. They look for reliability, fair treatment, and long-term relationships. A collaborative culture that values partnership and mutual benefit can enhance the efficiency and effectiveness of the supply chain. Organizations that cultivate strong relationships with their suppliers and partners can benefit from improved quality, innovation, and responsiveness, which are essential for successful strategy execution.

The community and society at large are increasingly recognized as important stakeholders, especially in the context of corporate social responsibility and sustainability. They expect organizations to contribute positively to social and environmental causes. A culture that prioritizes ethical behavior, social responsibility, and sustainability can enhance the organization's reputation and social license to operate. Engaging with the community and addressing societal concerns can lead to a more supportive external environment, which is conducive to achieving strategic objectives.

Regulatory bodies and government agencies, tasked with ensuring compliance and protecting public interests, also influence strategy execution. They expect organizations to adhere to laws, regulations, and standards. A culture of compliance, integrity, and transparency is essential to navigate the regulatory landscape effectively. Organizations that proactively engage with regulators and demonstrate a commitment to ethical practices can mitigate risks and avoid potential legal issues that could derail strategic plans.

In essence, the perspectives of various stakeholders are intertwined with the cultural fabric of an organization. By recognizing and addressing their diverse needs and expectations, organizations can create a business culture that not only supports but also drives successful strategy execution. Each stakeholder group brings unique insights and contributions that, when harmonized, can lead to a more resilient and adaptive organization capable of achieving its strategic goals.

Cultural Assessment Case Studies

In the bustling corridors of a global manufacturing company, the cultural underpinnings of corporate behavior become vividly apparent. Imagine a scene where a new CEO, hailing from a different continent, steps into an organization steeped in decades-old traditions. The CEO's mandate is clear: to transform the company's strategic direction and market positioning. However, the initial months reveal a deeper challenge beyond the strategic shifts – the ingrained cultural norms that resist change.

To understand the cultural landscape, the CEO initiates a comprehensive cultural assessment. This process involves structured interviews, surveys, and immersive observations aimed at uncovering the prevailing attitudes, values, and behaviors. The findings reveal a culture characterized by hierarchical decision-making, risk aversion, and a strong emphasis on process over innovation. Employees exhibit a deep respect for authority but are reluctant to voice dissent or propose radical ideas. This cultural backdrop poses a significant barrier to the CEO's vision of fostering agility and creative problem-solving.

The assessment extends to focus groups where employees from different levels and functions discuss their perceptions of the company's culture. These sessions uncover a dichotomy: while senior management believes the organization is adaptable and open to change, frontline employees feel stifled by rigid protocols and fear of retribution for mistakes. The cultural assessment highlights a disconnect between the leadership's perceptions and the everyday realities of the workforce.

In another case, a tech startup in Silicon Valley faces rapid growth and the ensuing cultural shifts that accompany scaling operations. Initially, the startup thrives on a culture of innovation, flat hierarchies, and open communication. However, as the company expands, the influx of new employees and the need for more structured processes begin to dilute the original culture. A cultural assessment is conducted to navigate this transitional phase.

The assessment reveals that while new hires bring diverse perspectives and skills, they also introduce varying expectations and work styles. Long-standing employees express concerns about losing the startup's entrepreneurial spirit and collaborative ethos. The assessment identifies key cultural attributes that need preservation and areas where integration of new practices is necessary. Workshops and team-building activities are recommended to bridge the cultural gaps and align the growing workforce with the company's core values.

Consider a multinational retail corporation grappling with underperformance in a specific regional market. The company's global culture emphasizes efficiency, customer-centricity, and innovation. However, the cultural assessment in the underperforming region uncovers a misalignment between the corporate culture and local market dynamics. Employees in this region face challenges in adopting global practices due to cultural nuances, such as differing communication styles and varying customer expectations.

The assessment process includes cultural immersion activities where corporate leaders spend time in local stores, interacting with employees and customers to gain firsthand insights. These interactions reveal the need for a more localized approach that respects regional cultural norms while maintaining the overarching corporate values. Tailored training programs and localized marketing strategies emerge as solutions to address the cultural misalignment and enhance market performance.

Through these case studies, the critical role of cultural assessments in strategy execution becomes evident. They serve as diagnostic tools that uncover the underlying cultural currents influencing organizational behavior. By identifying cultural barriers and facilitators, leaders can tailor their strategies to align with the existing cultural landscape or implement targeted interventions to drive cultural change. The nuanced understanding gained from cultural assessments enables organizations to navigate the complexities of global operations, ensuring that strategic initiatives resonate with and are supported by their cultural context.

Assessing and Diagnosing Your Current Culture

Organizational Factors	Current Culture	Desired Culture
Leadership Style	Top-down decision-making	Participative leadership
Communication	Limited communication	Open communication
Innovation	Risk-averse	Innovative mindset
Collaboration	Siloed departments	Cross-functional teamwork
Decision-Making	Centralized	Decentralized and inclusive

Chapter 04

Developing a Culture Change Strategy

Setting Cultural Change Objectives

In the intricate dance of strategy execution, the culture of an organization acts as both the rhythm and the melody. For businesses aiming to synchronize their operations with strategic goals, setting clear cultural change objectives becomes paramount. This process begins with a profound understanding of the existing culture and its alignment, or lack thereof, with the strategic vision.

The initial step involves a meticulous assessment of the current cultural landscape. Leaders must immerse themselves in the day-to-day realities of their organization, observing behaviors, listening to conversations, and analyzing the underlying values that drive actions. This phase is akin to diagnosing the health of the organization, identifying both strengths and areas that require transformation.

Once the cultural diagnosis is complete, the next task is to define the desired cultural state. This envisioned culture should be one that supports and propels the strategic objectives of the company. It is crucial to articulate this future state in concrete terms, describing specific behaviors, attitudes, and values that employees should embody. These descriptions serve as a north star, guiding the organization towards its strategic aspirations.

To ensure the cultural change objectives are not just aspirational but achievable, they must be SMART—Specific, Measurable, Achievable, Relevant, and Time-bound. Specificity in objectives helps in painting a clear picture of what the new culture looks like. Measurability ensures that progress can be tracked and assessed. Achievability keeps the goals within the realm of possibility, preventing disillusionment. Relevance ties the cultural objectives directly to strategic goals, ensuring they are pertinent. Time-bound objectives create a sense of urgency and momentum.

Engagement and buy-in from all levels of the organization are critical for successful cultural transformation. Leaders must communicate the cultural change objectives with clarity and conviction, highlighting the benefits for both the organization and its employees. This communication should be a two-way street, where feedback is actively sought and valued, fostering a sense of ownership and involvement among all stakeholders.

In parallel, identifying cultural champions within the organization can accelerate the change process. These individuals, who naturally embody the desired cultural traits, can influence and inspire their peers, serving as role models for the new cultural norms. Their stories and experiences can be powerful tools in illustrating the practical application of the cultural objectives.

Moreover, aligning the organizational systems and processes with the cultural change objectives is essential. Performance management systems, reward and recognition programs, and even recruitment practices should be reviewed and adjusted to reinforce the desired culture. This alignment ensures that the structural elements of the organization support and sustain the cultural transformation efforts.

Continuous monitoring and adaptation are also vital. The journey to cultural transformation is seldom linear; it requires ongoing assessment and flexibility. Regularly revisiting the cultural change objectives and measuring progress against them allows the organization to make necessary adjustments and keep the momentum alive.

By setting clear, actionable cultural change objectives, organizations lay the groundwork for a culture that not only aligns with but actively drives their strategic goals. This alignment fosters an environment where strategy execution becomes a natural outcome of the daily behaviors and decisions of every member of the organization. Through careful planning, communication, and consistent reinforcement, cultural change objectives can transform the very fabric of an organization, making strategy execution an inherent part of its DNA.

Engaging Employees in Cultural Change

Creating a successful business culture that aligns with strategic execution requires the active engagement of employees at every level. This engagement is not merely about informing staff of new initiatives but about fostering a deep, intrinsic connection to the organizational goals and values.

To achieve this, it is essential to begin by clearly communicating the vision and purpose behind the cultural change. Employees need to understand the 'why' before they can commit to the 'how.' This involves transparent and frequent communication from leadership, detailing how the cultural shift aligns with the overall strategic objectives of the company. Leaders should articulate the benefits that the change will bring, not just to the organization, but to the employees themselves. This could include improved work processes, better team collaboration, or enhanced personal development opportunities.

One effective method to engage employees is through storytelling. Sharing real-life examples and success stories can illustrate the positive impact of the cultural shift. These narratives should highlight individuals or teams who have already adopted the new cultural norms and have seen tangible benefits as a result. Storytelling can make the abstract concepts of cultural change more concrete and relatable, helping employees to visualize their own potential success within the new framework.

Involving employees in the process of cultural change is crucial. This can be achieved by soliciting their input and feedback through surveys, focus groups, or town hall meetings. When employees feel their voices are heard and their opinions matter, they are more likely to buy into the change. Additionally, involving employees in the planning and implementation stages can help to identify potential obstacles and areas of resistance early on, allowing for more effective problem-solving and smoother transitions.

Training and development programs are vital to equip employees with the skills and knowledge they need to thrive in the new culture. These programs should be tailored to address specific competencies that align with the desired cultural attributes. For example, if the cultural change emphasizes innovation, training might focus on creative thinking and problem-solving techniques. Continuous learning opportunities should be provided to reinforce the new cultural norms and ensure that the change is sustainable over the long term.

Recognition and reward systems play a significant role in reinforcing desired behaviors and attitudes. By acknowledging and celebrating employees who exemplify the new cultural values, organizations can create positive reinforcement loops. This could take the form of formal awards, public recognition in company communications, or even informal acknowledgments during team meetings. The key is to ensure that these rewards are consistent and aligned with the cultural attributes the organization is aiming to promote.

Leaders must lead by example. They should embody the cultural values in their daily actions and decisions, serving as role models for the rest of the organization. When employees see their leaders genuinely committed to the cultural change, they are more likely to follow suit. Leadership behavior sets the tone for the entire organization, and a consistent demonstration of the new cultural values can significantly accelerate the adoption process.

Ultimately, engaging employees in cultural change is about creating a shared sense of purpose and belonging. When employees feel connected to the organizational mission and see themselves as integral parts of the journey, they are more likely to contribute positively and proactively to the cultural transformation. This collective effort can drive the organization towards achieving its strategic objectives, fostering a cohesive and dynamic business culture.

Overcoming Resistance to Change

Navigating the complex landscape of organizational change can often feel like steering a ship through turbulent waters. Resistance to change is a natural reaction, deeply rooted in human psychology and organizational dynamics. Understanding the underlying reasons for this resistance is crucial for leaders aiming to implement strategic initiatives successfully.

One of the primary reasons employees resist change is fear of the unknown. When a new strategy is introduced, it disrupts established routines and creates uncertainty about the future. This fear can manifest as anxiety, skepticism, or even outright opposition. To mitigate these feelings, leaders must communicate openly and transparently about the reasons for the change, the benefits it will bring, and the steps involved in the transition. Providing a clear vision and detailed roadmap can help alleviate fears and build trust.

Another significant factor contributing to resistance is the perceived loss of control. Employees often feel that changes are imposed upon them without their input, leading to a sense of powerlessness. Involving employees in the change process can counteract this perception. By seeking their feedback, incorporating their suggestions, and giving them a role in the implementation, leaders can foster a sense of ownership and collaboration. This participatory approach not only reduces resistance but also enhances the quality of the change initiative by leveraging the collective insights and experiences of the workforce.

The existing organizational culture also plays a critical role in how change is received. A culture that values stability and tradition may be more resistant to change compared to one that embraces innovation and flexibility. Leaders need to assess the cultural readiness for change and, if necessary, work on shifting cultural norms and values to align with the new strategic direction. This might involve redefining success metrics, celebrating early adopters, and creating narratives that link the change to the organization's core values and mission.

Communication is the lifeblood of any change initiative. However, it's not just about the quantity of communication but the quality. Leaders must tailor their messages to different audiences within the organization, addressing specific concerns and highlighting relevant benefits. Consistent, honest, and empathetic communication helps build credibility and reduces the spread of rumors and misinformation. Regular updates and feedback loops ensure that employees feel informed and heard throughout the process.

Training and support are also essential in overcoming resistance. Change often requires new skills and behaviors, which can be daunting for employees. Providing comprehensive training programs, resources, and ongoing support helps ease the transition. Leaders should also recognize and reward efforts to adapt, reinforcing positive behavior and demonstrating the organization's commitment to supporting its workforce.

The pace of change can significantly impact resistance levels. While some changes may need to be implemented quickly, others benefit from a more gradual approach. Leaders must assess the urgency and scope of the change and plan the rollout accordingly. Phased implementation allows employees to adjust incrementally, reducing the shock and facilitating smoother adaptation.

Leadership behavior sets the tone for the entire organization. Leaders must model the change they wish to see, demonstrating commitment and resilience. Their actions and attitudes can either inspire confidence or exacerbate fears. By being visible, approachable, and supportive, leaders can galvanize their teams and drive the change forward.

In essence, overcoming resistance to change requires a multifaceted approach that addresses emotional, cognitive, and practical aspects. By understanding the root causes of resistance and proactively addressing them, leaders can transform potential obstacles into opportunities for growth and innovation.

Monitoring and Adjusting the Change Process

Change is an inevitable aspect of any business culture striving for effective strategy execution. The ability to monitor and adjust the change process is crucial to ensure that the organization remains on the right path towards achieving its strategic objectives. This involves a continuous cycle of observation, assessment, feedback, and realignment.

At the heart of monitoring the change process lies the establishment of clear metrics and key performance indicators (KPIs). These metrics serve as a compass, guiding the organization through the complexities of change. They provide tangible evidence of progress and highlight areas that require attention. KPIs should be aligned with the overall strategic goals and must be communicated effectively throughout the organization. Regular review meetings and progress reports ensure that everyone is aware of the current status and any necessary adjustments.

Employee feedback is another critical component in monitoring the change process. Employees are the ones who experience the changes firsthand, and their insights can be invaluable. Surveys, focus groups, and one-on-one interviews can provide deep insights into how the change is being perceived and implemented on the ground. This feedback loop not only helps in identifying potential issues early but also fosters a sense of involvement and ownership among employees.

Leadership plays a pivotal role in overseeing the change process. Leaders must be vigilant and proactive, continuously scanning the internal and external environment for any signs of deviation from the planned course. They must be prepared to make difficult decisions and adjustments to keep the organization aligned with its strategic goals. This could involve reallocating resources, revising timelines, or even altering the strategic plan itself in response to new information or changing circumstances.

Communication is the lifeblood of the change process. Transparent and consistent communication ensures that everyone in the organization understands the purpose of the change, the progress being made, and any adjustments that need to be implemented. This reduces uncertainty and resistance, making it easier for employees to adapt to new ways of working. Regular town hall meetings, newsletters, and intranet updates are effective tools for maintaining open lines of communication.

Technology can also play a significant role in monitoring and adjusting the change process. Advanced analytics and real-time data tracking allow for more precise monitoring of progress and quicker identification of issues. Project management software and collaboration tools can help in coordinating efforts and ensuring that everyone is on the same page.

The ability to adjust the change process is just as important as monitoring it. Flexibility and adaptability are key attributes that organizations must cultivate. When discrepancies or challenges are identified, swift and decisive action is required. This might involve revising strategies, reallocating resources, or even changing leadership if necessary. The goal is to remain agile and responsive, ensuring that the organization can pivot as needed to stay aligned with its strategic objectives.

Training and development programs can support the adjustment process by equipping employees with the skills and knowledge they need to adapt to new roles and responsibilities. Continuous learning opportunities foster a culture of resilience and adaptability, enabling the organization to navigate the complexities of change more effectively.

By integrating these elements, businesses can create a robust framework for monitoring and adjusting the change process. This not only ensures that the organization remains on track but also builds a resilient and adaptable business culture capable of executing its strategy effectively.

Chapter 05

Building a Culture of Innovation

Encouraging Creativity and Risk-Taking

A bustling office space filled with the hum of activity, where ideas flow as freely as the coffee, sets the stage for a thriving business culture. The walls are adorned with vibrant artwork, each piece a testament to the company's commitment to fostering creativity. Employees, dressed in a mix of casual and business attire, huddle in small groups, their faces animated with excitement as they brainstorm innovative solutions to complex problems. The atmosphere is one of palpable energy and possibility, where every voice is heard and every idea is valued.

In this dynamic environment, leaders play a pivotal role in cultivating a culture that encourages creativity and risk-taking. They understand that innovation is the lifeblood of any successful organization and that it thrives in a space where employees feel safe to experiment and challenge the status quo. Leaders are not just figureheads but active participants in the creative process, often rolling up their sleeves to collaborate with their teams. They lead by example, demonstrating a willingness to take calculated risks and learn from failures.

The physical space of the office is designed to inspire. Open floor plans with flexible seating arrangements allow for spontaneous interactions and the free exchange of ideas. Whiteboards and sticky notes are ubiquitous, serving as canvases for the team's collective imagination. Quiet zones and creative nooks provide employees with the solitude needed for deep thinking, while communal areas foster collaboration and camaraderie. This thoughtfully curated environment signals to employees that their creativity is not only welcomed but essential.

Formal structures are in place to support creative endeavors. Regular innovation workshops and hackathons are organized, offering employees a platform to pitch their ideas and receive constructive feedback. These events are not just about generating new concepts but also about building a culture of continuous improvement and learning. Mentorship programs pair seasoned professionals with newcomers, creating a rich tapestry of knowledge and experience that fuels innovation. Leaders are approachable and accessible, often holding open-door hours where employees can discuss their ideas and seek guidance.

Risk-taking is celebrated as a vital component of the creative process. Employees are encouraged to step out of their comfort zones and explore uncharted territories. Failures are not met with reprimand but with a spirit of inquiry and understanding. Post-mortem meetings are a common practice, where teams dissect what went wrong and extract valuable lessons for future endeavors. This approach transforms failures into opportunities for growth, reinforcing the notion that taking risks is an integral part of achieving success.

Recognition and rewards are tailored to celebrate creative achievements and bold initiatives. Whether it's a shout-out in a company-wide meeting, a feature in the internal newsletter, or tangible rewards like bonuses and promotions, employees know that their contributions are valued. This recognition serves as a powerful motivator, inspiring others to push the boundaries of their creativity.

The company invests in continuous learning and development, offering workshops, courses, and access to industry conferences. Employees are encouraged to pursue their passions and expand their skill sets. This commitment to personal and professional growth creates a workforce that is not only skilled but also deeply engaged and motivated.

In this vibrant business culture, creativity and risk-taking are not just encouraged but are integral to the organization's DNA. This environment equips employees with the confidence and resources they need to innovate, driving the company toward sustained success and a competitive edge in the marketplace.

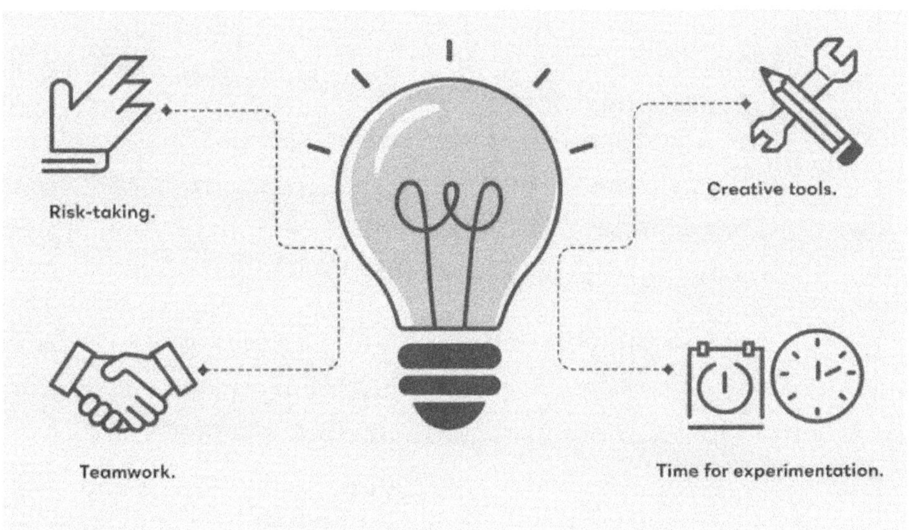

Structures and Processes that Foster Innovation

To catalyze the successful execution of strategy within a business, it is imperative to establish structures and processes that foster innovation. These elements serve as the backbone for a vibrant culture where creativity and forward-thinking are not just encouraged but systematically ingrained into the daily operations of the organization.

A key structure that supports innovation is a dedicated team or department focused on research and development (R&D). This unit operates as a crucible for new ideas, providing the resources and environment necessary for experimentation and discovery. By isolating a segment of the workforce to concentrate solely on innovation, businesses can ensure that there is a continuous pipeline of fresh concepts and approaches ready to be integrated into the broader strategic framework.

Cross-functional teams also play a crucial role. These teams bring together individuals from diverse departments—such as marketing, engineering, finance, and customer service—to collaborate on projects. The melding of different perspectives and expertise often leads to more holistic and innovative solutions, as it allows for the cross-pollination of ideas. The synergy generated within these teams can break down silos and promote a culture of open communication and shared goals.

Processes that support innovation are equally vital. One such process is the implementation of an idea management system. This system provides a structured way for employees at all levels to submit, track, and develop their ideas. By creating a transparent and accessible platform for idea generation, businesses can tap into the collective creativity of their workforce. Incentive programs linked to this system can further motivate employees to contribute their best ideas.

Another important process is the establishment of a feedback loop that integrates customer insights into the innovation cycle. Regularly gathering and analyzing customer feedback ensures that the company remains attuned to market needs and can adapt its strategies accordingly. This customer-centric approach not only fosters innovation but also enhances customer satisfaction and loyalty.

Agile methodologies are also instrumental in fostering innovation. These methodologies emphasize iterative development, where projects are broken down into smaller, manageable segments that are continuously tested and refined. This approach allows for rapid prototyping and quick adjustments based on real-world feedback, enabling the organization to stay nimble and responsive to change.

Leadership commitment to innovation is a crucial driver. Leaders must not only advocate for innovation but also model it through their actions. By prioritizing innovation in strategic planning and resource allocation, leaders can signal its importance to the entire organization. Furthermore, they should foster an environment where failure is viewed as a learning opportunity rather than a setback, thereby encouraging risk-taking and experimentation.

Training and development programs aimed at enhancing creative thinking and problem-solving skills are also essential. These programs equip employees with the tools and techniques needed to think outside the box and approach challenges from new angles. By investing in the continuous development of their workforce, businesses can maintain a competitive edge in the ever-evolving marketplace.

In essence, the structures and processes that foster innovation are multifaceted and interdependent. They require a deliberate and sustained effort to cultivate, but the payoff is substantial. A culture that prioritizes and systematically supports innovation is one that is well-positioned to execute its strategy effectively and achieve long-term success.

Recognizing and Rewarding Innovation

Within the realm of strategic execution, fostering an environment where innovation is not only encouraged but actively rewarded becomes crucial. This atmosphere of recognition acts as a catalyst, propelling employees to push boundaries and think outside conventional paradigms. By acknowledging creative efforts and successes, businesses can cultivate a culture that values forward-thinking ideas and continuous improvement.

Innovation thrives in environments where employees feel their contributions are valued. When a company publicly celebrates innovative achievements, it sends a powerful message: creativity is essential and appreciated. This recognition can take many forms, ranging from formal awards and public acknowledgments to more personalized gestures such as handwritten notes or one-on-one meetings with senior leadership. The key is to ensure that the recognition is sincere and meaningful, resonating with the recipients and inspiring others to follow suit.

Monetary rewards, though effective, are not the only means to incentivize innovation. Offering opportunities for career advancement, professional development, and increased autonomy can be equally motivating. Employees who see a clear path for growth within the organization are more likely to invest their creative energies in projects that align with the company's strategic goals. This alignment not only enhances individual satisfaction and engagement but also drives the collective success of the organization.

Creating a structured system for recognizing and rewarding innovation helps maintain consistency and fairness. Establishing clear criteria for what constitutes innovative behavior ensures that all employees understand the expectations and the potential rewards.

These criteria should be communicated transparently and reviewed regularly to adapt to the evolving landscape of the business and its strategic objectives.

In addition to formal recognition programs, fostering a culture of continuous feedback and open communication is essential. Encouraging managers and peers to provide regular, constructive feedback helps employees understand how their innovative efforts are perceived and where improvements can be made. This ongoing dialogue not only nurtures a supportive environment but also helps identify potential obstacles to innovation early, allowing for timely interventions.

Celebrating small wins is as important as recognizing major breakthroughs. Innovation often involves incremental improvements and learning from failures. By acknowledging these smaller achievements, businesses can maintain momentum and keep employees motivated. This approach also reinforces the notion that innovation is a continuous process, not a one-time event.

Leadership plays a pivotal role in setting the tone for innovation recognition. Leaders who actively participate in recognizing and rewarding innovative efforts demonstrate their commitment to fostering a culture of creativity. Their involvement can range from participating in award ceremonies to personally congratulating employees for their achievements. This visible support from the top echelons of the organization reinforces the importance of innovation and encourages employees at all levels to contribute their ideas.

Another critical aspect of recognizing and rewarding innovation is ensuring that the process is inclusive. All employees, regardless of their role or department, should have the opportunity to be recognized for their innovative contributions. This inclusivity helps break down silos and encourages cross-functional collaboration, leading to more holistic and impactful innovations.

By embedding recognition and rewards into the fabric of the organizational culture, businesses can create a sustainable environment where innovation flourishes. This culture not only attracts top talent but also retains and engages existing employees, driving long-term success. The continuous cycle of recognition, reward, and innovation becomes a powerful engine for strategic execution, enabling businesses to adapt and thrive in an ever-changing landscape.

Case Studies of Innovative Cultures

In the realm of business, the synergy between culture and strategy is a crucial determinant of organizational success. Examining real-world examples can illuminate how innovative cultures serve as the bedrock for effective strategy execution. Consider the case of Google, a company renowned for its unique and forward-thinking culture. Google's commitment to fostering a culture of innovation is evident through its "20% time" policy, where employees are encouraged to dedicate a portion of their work hours to projects they are passionate about. This initiative has led to the creation of groundbreaking products like Gmail and Google News, underscoring the importance of giving employees the freedom to explore and innovate.

Another exemplary case is Netflix, which has built a culture centered around freedom and responsibility. Netflix's approach to employee management is unconventional; there are no fixed working hours, and the company offers unlimited vacation days. This trust-based model empowers employees to take ownership of their work, leading to high levels of accountability and creativity. The result is a dynamic environment where innovation thrives, enabling Netflix to continuously adapt to market changes and remain a leader in the entertainment industry.

3M provides another compelling example with its long-standing tradition of innovation. The company's "15% rule" allows employees to spend a portion of their time on projects that are not part of their regular job duties. This policy has been instrumental in the development of some of 3M's most successful products, such as Post-it Notes and Scotchgard. By cultivating a culture that values experimentation and risk-taking, 3M has maintained its competitive edge and sustained growth over the decades.

Atlassian, a software company known for its collaborative tools like Jira and Confluence, emphasizes the importance of continuous improvement and learning. The company's "ShipIt" days are a testament to this philosophy, where employees are given 24 hours to work on any project they choose, with the aim of delivering a tangible product by the end of the period. These hackathon-style events not only foster creativity but also strengthen team collaboration, resulting in innovative solutions that drive the company's success.

Tesla, under the leadership of Elon Musk, exemplifies a culture of relentless innovation and ambition. The company's mission to accelerate the world's transition to sustainable energy is mirrored in its organizational culture, which encourages employees to challenge the status quo and push the boundaries of what is possible. Tesla's flat organizational structure facilitates open communication and rapid decision-making, enabling the company to innovate at a pace that sets it apart from traditional automakers.

Zappos, an online shoe and clothing retailer, places a strong emphasis on customer service and employee happiness. The company's unique culture is built around ten core values that guide every aspect of its operations. Zappos' dedication to maintaining a positive and empowering work environment has resulted in high employee satisfaction and exceptional customer service, contributing to its sustained success in a competitive market.

These case studies illustrate that a culture of innovation is not a one-size-fits-all concept. Each organization has tailored its cultural practices to align with its strategic goals and industry demands. Whether through policies that encourage creative freedom, trust-based management models, or continuous learning initiatives, these companies demonstrate that fostering an innovative culture is integral to successful strategy execution.

Chapter 06

Fostering a Collaborative Work Environment

The Importance of Collaboration

Within the intricate tapestry of business culture, the threads of collaboration are woven with paramount significance. Here, the synergy of minds converges, creating a harmonious environment where strategy execution thrives. The essence of collaboration lies not merely in the act of working together, but in the profound connection and mutual respect that underpins it. This connection fosters an atmosphere where ideas can flourish, and innovations are born from the collective intelligence of a unified team.

In the bustling corridors of modern enterprises, the spirit of collaboration is palpable. It manifests in the open dialogues that occur in meeting rooms, the spontaneous brainstorming sessions in casual settings, and the seamless integration of diverse perspectives. This culture of collaboration is not confined to hierarchical structures; it permeates every level, encouraging a free flow of ideas from all corners of the organization. The power of collaboration is such that it transforms individual efforts into a cohesive force, driving the organization towards its strategic goals with a shared vision.

In the realm of strategy execution, collaboration acts as a catalyst, accelerating progress and ensuring alignment across various functions. When teams collaborate effectively, they break down silos that often hinder communication and impede the flow of information. This interconnectedness allows for a more agile response to challenges and opportunities, as insights and feedback are rapidly disseminated and acted upon. The collective problem-solving capability of a collaborative team often leads to innovative solutions that might not emerge in isolation.

Moreover, collaboration fosters a sense of ownership and accountability among team members. When individuals feel that their contributions are valued and that they are part of a larger mission, their commitment to the organization's objectives deepens. This shared responsibility is critical for the execution of strategies, as it ensures that everyone is working towards the same goals with a unified purpose. The alignment of efforts and the pooling of diverse skills and knowledge result in a more robust and resilient execution of strategies.

The importance of collaboration is further highlighted in the context of a rapidly changing business landscape. In an era where adaptability and speed are crucial, the ability to collaborate effectively becomes a competitive advantage. Organizations that cultivate a collaborative culture are better positioned to navigate uncertainties and pivot when necessary. The collective agility of a collaborative team enables swift decision-making and the ability to implement strategies with precision and confidence.

Furthermore, collaboration nurtures a culture of continuous learning and improvement. When team members collaborate, they share their experiences, learn from each other, and collectively refine their approaches. This ongoing exchange of knowledge and skills enhances the overall competence of the team, making them more adept at executing strategies. The openness to feedback and the willingness to learn from both successes and failures contribute to a dynamic and evolving business culture.

In essence, the importance of collaboration in business culture cannot be overstated. It is the bedrock upon which successful strategy execution is built. By fostering an environment where collaboration is encouraged and nurtured, organizations can harness the full potential of their teams. The collective intelligence, creativity, and commitment that emerge from a collaborative culture drive the organization forward, ensuring that strategic goals are not only met but exceeded.

Building Trust and Open Communication

Trust forms the bedrock of any successful organization, and nowhere is this more evident than in the realm of strategy execution. Trust fosters an environment where employees feel safe to share ideas, take risks, and collaborate without fear of retribution. It is the invisible glue that binds teams together, enabling them to work efficiently and harmoniously towards common goals.

Open communication is the lifeblood that keeps this trust alive. When communication flows freely and transparently, misunderstandings are minimized, and alignment is maintained. Leaders play a crucial role in setting the tone for open communication. Their willingness to listen, share information, and engage in honest dialogue sets an example for the entire organization. When leaders are transparent about the company's goals, challenges, and decisions, they build credibility and foster a culture of trust.

The physical and virtual spaces within an organization also impact the level of trust and openness. Open office layouts, for instance, can break down hierarchical barriers and encourage spontaneous interactions. However, these spaces must be complemented by virtual platforms that facilitate continuous and inclusive communication, especially in today's digital age. Tools such as intranets, chat applications, and video conferencing can bridge the gap between different departments and geographical locations, ensuring that everyone stays connected and informed.

Building trust and open communication is not solely the responsibility of leaders. Every member of the organization must contribute to this culture. Employees should feel empowered to voice their thoughts and concerns without fear of negative repercussions.

This requires a shift from a blame culture to a learning culture, where mistakes are seen as opportunities for growth rather than failures. Constructive feedback should be encouraged and valued, as it helps individuals and teams to improve and innovate.

Trust and open communication also have a significant impact on employee engagement and retention. When employees trust their leaders and feel heard, they are more likely to be committed to their work and the organization. This sense of belonging and purpose can drive higher levels of productivity and creativity, which are essential for effective strategy execution.

Regular check-ins and feedback sessions can help maintain this culture. These interactions should be more than just formal performance reviews; they should be opportunities for genuine dialogue and connection. Leaders should ask open-ended questions, listen actively, and show empathy. This not only helps in identifying potential issues early but also strengthens the bond between leaders and their teams.

Moreover, recognizing and celebrating achievements, both big and small, can reinforce trust and motivation. Public acknowledgment of individual and team contributions shows that their efforts are valued and appreciated. This positive reinforcement can inspire others to strive for excellence and collaborate more effectively.

In times of change or crisis, the importance of trust and open communication becomes even more pronounced. Transparent communication about the reasons for change, its implications, and the steps being taken to address challenges can alleviate uncertainty and build resilience. Trust in leadership and the organizational direction can help navigate through turbulent times with greater cohesion and confidence.

Ultimately, the cultivation of trust and open communication requires consistent effort and commitment from everyone in the organization. It is a continuous process that evolves with the organization's growth and changing dynamics. By prioritizing these values, organizations can create a strong foundation for effective strategy execution and long-term success.

Collaborative Tools and Technologies

The modern business landscape is characterized by rapid change, necessitating that organizations adapt quickly to maintain a competitive edge. One critical factor in achieving this agility is the effective use of collaborative tools and technologies. These innovations have revolutionized the way teams interact, share information, and execute strategies.

Within the realm of collaborative tools, digital communication platforms have become indispensable. Tools such as Slack, Microsoft Teams, and Zoom facilitate real-time communication, enabling team members to connect regardless of geographical location. These platforms support text, voice, and video interactions, ensuring that complex ideas can be communicated clearly and promptly. Additionally, integrated features like file sharing, screen sharing, and collaborative document editing streamline workflows and minimize the time spent on administrative tasks.

Project management software has also transformed strategic execution. Applications such as Asana, Trello, and Monday.com allow teams to visualize tasks, set deadlines, and track progress in a transparent manner. These tools provide a centralized platform where all project-related information is stored, making it easy for team members to stay informed and aligned with project goals. By offering features like task assignment, progress tracking, and milestone setting, project management software ensures that everyone is on the same page, reducing the risk of miscommunication and delays.

Cloud-based storage solutions play a pivotal role in supporting collaboration. Services like Google Drive, Dropbox, and OneDrive offer secure, scalable storage options that can be accessed from any device with an internet connection. These platforms facilitate the sharing of large files and enable real-time collaboration on documents, spreadsheets, and presentations. The ability to access and edit files remotely ensures that team members can contribute to projects without being confined to a specific location, promoting flexibility and efficiency.

Collaborative technologies also extend to specialized tools tailored for specific business functions. For instance, customer relationship management (CRM) systems like Salesforce and HubSpot integrate sales, marketing, and customer service efforts, providing a holistic view of customer interactions. These platforms enable teams to collaborate on customer strategies, share insights, and track the impact of their efforts. Similarly, enterprise resource planning (ERP) systems such as SAP and Oracle facilitate collaboration across different departments by integrating various business processes into a single platform.

The adoption of collaborative tools is not without challenges. Organizations must ensure that their digital infrastructure is robust enough to support these technologies. Additionally, there is a need for comprehensive training programs to help employees become proficient in using these tools. Security concerns also arise, requiring stringent measures to protect sensitive information from cyber threats.

Despite these challenges, the benefits of collaborative tools and technologies are undeniable. They enhance communication, streamline workflows, and foster a culture of transparency and accountability. By leveraging these tools, organizations can execute their strategies more effectively, respond to market changes swiftly, and maintain a high level of productivity.

The integration of collaborative tools into business processes represents a significant shift in how organizations operate. These technologies not only facilitate the execution of strategies but also empower employees to work more cohesively and innovatively. As businesses continue to evolve, the role of collaborative tools and technologies will undoubtedly become even more critical in shaping successful strategy execution.

Examples of Collaborative Cultures

In dynamic work environments where strategy execution is key, collaborative cultures serve as the linchpin for achieving objectives. One notable example is found in tech giants like Google. At Google, collaboration is not merely encouraged but embedded in the company's DNA. Open office spaces, cross-functional teams, and a culture that promotes psychological safety allow for the free exchange of ideas. Employees are encouraged to take risks and share innovative concepts without the fear of ridicule or harsh criticism. This approach fosters a sense of belonging and mutual respect, driving the collective effort towards the company's strategic goals.

Another compelling example is Toyota's renowned production system. Built on the principles of continuous improvement and respect for people, Toyota's collaborative culture emphasizes teamwork and collective problem-solving. The practice of "genchi genbutsu," or "go and see for yourself," empowers employees at all levels to identify issues on the ground and collaborate on solutions. This hands-on approach ensures that problems are not just escalated but resolved collaboratively, contributing to the seamless execution of strategic initiatives.

In the healthcare sector, the Mayo Clinic stands out for its collaborative culture. Physicians, nurses, and administrative staff work in integrated teams, putting patient care at the forefront of their activities. The Clinic's model ensures that diverse expertise is brought together to diagnose and treat patients, fostering an environment where collaboration is not just beneficial but essential. This collective approach to healthcare delivery ensures that strategic decisions are made with comprehensive input, leading to better patient outcomes and organizational efficiency.

Retail giant Zappos offers another perspective on collaborative culture. Known for its unique corporate ethos, Zappos emphasizes employee happiness and customer satisfaction. The company's holacratic structure eliminates traditional hierarchies, promoting a more inclusive and collaborative environment. Employees are given the autonomy to make decisions and are encouraged to work together across different roles and departments. This culture of collaboration not only enhances employee satisfaction but also aligns with the company's strategic aim of delivering exceptional customer service.

In the realm of nonprofit organizations, Habitat for Humanity exemplifies a collaborative culture that drives strategic execution. Volunteers, staff, and community members come together to build homes for those in need. The organization's success hinges on the collective effort and shared vision of its diverse stakeholders. Collaborative planning sessions, community involvement, and volunteer engagement are integral to Habitat for Humanity's strategy, ensuring that every project is executed with a unified purpose.

Within the financial sector, Goldman Sachs showcases a collaborative culture that balances competition with teamwork. While individual performance is recognized, the firm places significant emphasis on collaborative success. Cross-departmental projects and mentorship programs are designed to foster a culture where knowledge sharing and teamwork are paramount. This collaborative environment supports the firm's strategic initiatives by leveraging the collective expertise and insights of its workforce.

These examples illustrate that collaborative cultures can take various forms, tailored to the unique needs and strategic goals of each organization. Whether it's through open communication, integrated teams, or inclusive decision-making processes, the common thread is the emphasis on collective effort and shared success. Organizations that cultivate such cultures are better positioned to execute their strategies effectively, harnessing the power of collaboration to navigate challenges and seize opportunities.

Chapter 07

Aligning Culture with Business Goals

Translating Strategic Goals into Cultural Practices

Business Culture for Strategy Execution

The alignment of strategic goals with cultural practices is a delicate and complex endeavor that requires a deep understanding of both the explicit and implicit elements that drive organizational behavior. To begin with, strategic goals are often articulated in clear, measurable terms, such as increasing market share, enhancing customer satisfaction, or driving innovation. These goals are typically outlined in strategic plans, annual reports, and executive presentations. However, the translation of these high-level objectives into day-to-day actions involves a nuanced interplay of values, beliefs, and rituals that constitute the organization's culture.

Cultural practices, unlike strategic goals, are not always documented or formally communicated. They are the unwritten rules and shared understandings that guide how employees interact, make decisions, and prioritize their work. These practices are often deeply rooted in the history and identity of the organization, making them resistant to change. Therefore, to effectively translate strategic goals into cultural practices, leaders must first diagnose the existing culture and identify the gaps between current behaviors and desired outcomes.

One effective approach is to conduct cultural assessments, which can include surveys, focus groups, and interviews with employees at all levels. These assessments help to uncover the underlying assumptions and values that drive behavior within the organization. For instance, if a company's strategic goal is to foster innovation, but the cultural assessment reveals a risk-averse mindset, there is a clear misalignment that needs to be addressed. In such cases, leaders might need to promote a culture of experimentation and learning, where failure is seen as a valuable part of the innovation process.

Another critical aspect is the role of leadership in modeling and reinforcing the desired cultural practices. Leaders must embody the values and behaviors that align with the strategic goals. This involves more than just verbal endorsements; it requires consistent actions that demonstrate commitment to the desired culture. For example, if collaboration is a strategic priority, leaders should actively participate in cross-functional teams, recognize collaborative efforts, and ensure that performance metrics reward teamwork as much as individual achievements.

Communication is also a vital tool in aligning cultural practices with strategic goals. Clear, consistent, and transparent communication helps to bridge the gap between high-level objectives and everyday actions. This can be achieved through various channels, such as town hall meetings, internal newsletters, and digital platforms, where leaders can share stories of how employees are living the desired values and contributing to strategic goals. These narratives not only provide tangible examples but also create a sense of shared purpose and community.

Training and development programs can further support the alignment process by equipping employees with the skills and knowledge needed to enact the desired cultural practices. Workshops, seminars, and e-learning modules can focus on areas such as leadership development, change management, and cultural competence. By investing in employee development, organizations signal their commitment to aligning culture with strategy, thereby fostering an environment where strategic goals are more likely to be achieved.

Finally, the alignment of strategic goals with cultural practices should be an ongoing process, not a one-time initiative. Regular reviews and adjustments are necessary to ensure that the culture evolves in tandem with the strategic direction of the organization. Feedback mechanisms, such as employee surveys and performance reviews, can provide valuable insights into the effectiveness of cultural initiatives and highlight areas for improvement.

In essence, translating strategic goals into cultural practices involves a comprehensive and continuous effort to align the visible and invisible elements of organizational life. By understanding the existing culture, modeling desired behaviors, communicating effectively, investing in development, and maintaining ongoing alignment, organizations can create a cohesive environment where strategic goals are not only articulated but also realized.

Strategic Goal	Cultural Practice
Increase Market Share	Encourage Cross-team Collaboration
Enhance Customer Satisfaction	Foster a Customer-centric Mindset
Drive Innovation	Promote Creative Problem-solving
Improve Employee Retention	Recognize and Reward Employee Engagement
Expand into New Markets	Cultivate Adaptability and Flexibility
Improve Operational Efficiency	Encourage Open Communication and Feedback

Creating Cultural Metrics and KPIs

To effectively align an organization's culture with its strategic goals, it becomes imperative to create robust cultural metrics and key performance indicators (KPIs). These tools enable leaders to measure the intangible aspects of culture that significantly influence performance and strategy execution. The first step in developing these metrics is to understand the core values and behaviors that define the desired organizational culture. These elements should resonate with the strategic objectives and be communicated clearly across all levels of the organization.

A critical aspect of this process is identifying the specific cultural attributes that drive success. For instance, if innovation is a strategic priority, the organization needs to measure how well its culture supports creative thinking and risk-taking. This can be done through surveys that assess employees' perceptions of their freedom to experiment and the support they receive for new ideas. Similarly, if customer satisfaction is a key goal, metrics might focus on how well the culture fosters a customer-centric mindset among employees.

Once the relevant cultural attributes are identified, the next step is to develop KPIs that provide quantitative and qualitative data on these attributes. Quantitative KPIs might include metrics such as employee engagement scores, turnover rates, and the frequency of cross-functional collaboration. These indicators offer a numerical snapshot of the cultural health of the organization. Qualitative KPIs, on the other hand, might involve narrative feedback from employees, insights from exit interviews, and case studies of successful cultural initiatives. These qualitative measures provide depth and context to the quantitative data, offering a more comprehensive understanding of cultural dynamics.

The process of creating cultural metrics and KPIs involves collaboration across various departments, including human resources, operations, and strategic planning. This cross-functional approach ensures that the metrics are relevant and aligned with the broader organizational strategy. Additionally, involving diverse perspectives in the development of these metrics helps to capture the multifaceted nature of culture, which cannot be fully understood through a single lens.

Moreover, it is crucial to establish a baseline for these metrics to track progress over time. This baseline provides a reference point against which future data can be compared, allowing leaders to identify trends and make informed decisions about cultural interventions. Regular monitoring and reporting of these metrics ensure that culture remains a visible and integral part of the strategic conversation.

An essential element of this process is transparency. Sharing the results of cultural assessments and KPIs with employees fosters a sense of collective responsibility and engagement. It also provides an opportunity for open dialogue about cultural strengths and areas for improvement. When employees see that their feedback is valued and acted upon, it reinforces their commitment to the desired cultural attributes.

Incorporating cultural metrics and KPIs into performance reviews and strategic planning sessions ensures that culture is not treated as an abstract concept but as a tangible factor that directly impacts organizational success. Leaders can use these metrics to identify gaps between the current and desired culture and to develop targeted initiatives to bridge these gaps. This continuous cycle of measurement, feedback, and improvement helps to embed the desired culture deeply within the organizational fabric.

By systematically measuring and managing culture through well-defined metrics and KPIs, organizations can create a strong foundation for effective strategy execution. This approach not only aligns cultural attributes with strategic goals but also fosters a resilient and adaptive organizational environment capable of navigating the complexities of the modern business landscape.

Continuous Alignment and Realignment

In the ever-evolving landscape of business, the alignment and realignment of organizational elements are not merely tasks but essential continuous processes. Organizations that excel in strategy execution understand the importance of maintaining a dynamic equilibrium between their strategic objectives and operational activities. This ongoing calibration ensures that every part of the organization remains in sync with its overarching goals, fostering agility and resilience in the face of change.

The process begins with a clear understanding of the organization's vision and mission, which serve as the North Star guiding all strategic initiatives. Leaders play a pivotal role in communicating these elements effectively across all levels of the organization. This communication must be more than a one-time event; it requires regular reinforcement through various channels such as meetings, newsletters, and performance reviews. By doing so, leaders ensure that every team member, from the C-suite to the front lines, remains aligned with the strategic direction.

Once the vision and mission are well-communicated, the next step involves aligning the organizational culture with these strategic imperatives. Culture, often described as the organization's DNA, influences how employees think, behave, and make decisions. A culture that supports strategic goals can significantly enhance execution, while a misaligned culture can hinder progress. Therefore, leaders must assess and, if necessary, reshape the culture to foster behaviors that align with strategic objectives. This might involve introducing new values, redefining existing ones, or even changing certain long-standing practices.

Performance management systems are another critical component in this alignment process. These systems should be designed to measure and reward behaviors that contribute to strategic goals. Key Performance Indicators (KPIs) and other metrics must be regularly reviewed and updated to reflect the evolving strategic landscape. This ensures that employees are not only aware of what is expected of them but are also motivated to contribute effectively to the organization's success.

Technology plays an increasingly important role in facilitating continuous alignment and realignment. Advanced data analytics and business intelligence tools provide real-time insights into various aspects of the organization, from financial performance to customer satisfaction. These insights enable leaders to make informed decisions quickly, adjusting strategies and operations as needed to maintain alignment. Moreover, digital platforms can enhance communication and collaboration across different departments, breaking down silos that often hinder effective strategy execution.

Employee engagement is another crucial element. Engaged employees are more likely to understand and commit to the organization's strategic goals. Regular feedback loops, town hall meetings, and employee surveys can provide valuable insights into how well the organization is aligned and where adjustments might be needed. Leaders should not only seek feedback but also act on it, demonstrating a commitment to continuous improvement.

Flexibility and adaptability are essential traits for organizations striving for continuous alignment. The business environment is characterized by rapid changes, from technological advancements to shifts in consumer behavior. Organizations must be prepared to pivot and realign their strategies and operations in response to these changes. This requires a mindset that views change not as a disruption but as an opportunity for growth and innovation.

In essence, continuous alignment and realignment are about creating a dynamic, responsive organization that can adapt to changing circumstances while staying true to its core strategic objectives. It involves a holistic approach that encompasses leadership, culture, performance management, technology, and employee engagement. By fostering an environment where alignment is an ongoing process, organizations can enhance their ability to execute strategies effectively, ultimately achieving sustained success in a competitive marketplace.

Success Stories of Aligned Cultures

The vibrant synergy between organizational culture and strategy execution can be seen vividly through various success stories across different industries. When companies align their internal cultures with their strategic goals, the results often transcend expectations, leading to remarkable achievements and sustainable growth. These narratives serve as compelling evidence of how a well-aligned culture can be a formidable catalyst for success.

Take the example of Zappos, an online shoe and clothing retailer renowned for its exceptional customer service. Zappos' culture, deeply rooted in delivering happiness to customers, employees, and vendors, is not just a set of values written on the wall. It is a lived reality, reflected in every interaction and decision. The company empowers its employees to go above and beyond in serving customers, fostering a culture where people are motivated to provide extraordinary service. This alignment between culture and strategic focus on customer satisfaction has propelled Zappos to the forefront of the e-commerce industry, setting a gold standard for customer experience.

Another illustrative case is Southwest Airlines, whose culture of employee empowerment, humor, and customer service has been instrumental in its sustained profitability in the highly competitive airline industry. Southwest's strategic emphasis on cost efficiency and customer satisfaction is mirrored in its culture, where employees are encouraged to be themselves and make decisions that benefit the customer. This cultural alignment has not only led to a loyal customer base but also to operational efficiencies and a strong, engaged workforce.

Patagonia, the outdoor clothing and gear company, offers a different yet equally compelling story. Patagonia's commitment to environmental sustainability and ethical business practices is deeply ingrained in its culture. This alignment is evident in their strategic initiatives, such as the "Worn Wear" program that encourages customers to repair and reuse products instead of buying new ones. The company's culture of environmental stewardship resonates with its customer base, enhancing brand loyalty and driving growth. Patagonia's success demonstrates how a strong, value-driven culture can align with and propel a company's strategic objectives.

Toyota provides another noteworthy example with its culture of continuous improvement, known as "Kaizen." This philosophy encourages every employee, from assembly line workers to executives, to seek ways to improve processes and products. Toyota's strategic focus on quality and efficiency is intrinsically linked to this cultural ethos. The result is a history of innovation, high-quality products, and a reputation for reliability that has made Toyota a leader in the automotive industry.

Google's culture of innovation and openness has also played a critical role in its strategic success. The company fosters an environment where creativity and experimentation are encouraged, and failure is seen as a learning opportunity. This cultural alignment with Google's strategic focus on innovation has led to groundbreaking products and services, from the search engine itself to platforms like Android and innovations in artificial intelligence.

These success stories highlight the transformative power of aligning organizational culture with strategic goals. When employees understand and embrace the company's mission and values, their collective efforts can drive extraordinary outcomes. The key lies in fostering a culture that not only supports but actively drives the strategic objectives of the organization. Through these examples, it becomes evident that a well-aligned culture is not just an asset but a fundamental driver of long-term success and competitive advantage.

Chapter 08

The Impact of Globalization on Business Culture

Cultural Diversity in Global Organizations

In today's interconnected world, businesses operate on a global stage, where cultural diversity plays a pivotal role in shaping organizational dynamics. Global organizations encounter a rich tapestry of cultures, each contributing unique perspectives, values, and practices. This diversity, while presenting challenges, also offers immense opportunities for innovation and growth. Understanding and leveraging cultural diversity is essential for effective strategy execution in multinational enterprises.

Diverse cultural backgrounds influence how employees perceive authority, approach problem-solving, and communicate. For instance, hierarchical cultures, such as those in many Asian countries, may emphasize respect for authority and seniority, while more egalitarian cultures, like those in Northern Europe, promote equality and open dialogue. These differences can impact decision-making processes, leadership styles, and team dynamics. Recognizing and adapting to these variations allows organizations to foster a more inclusive and cohesive work environment.

Communication styles vary significantly across cultures. High-context cultures, such as Japan and China, rely heavily on non-verbal cues and the context of the conversation, whereas low-context cultures, like the United States and Germany, prioritize direct and explicit communication. Misunderstandings can arise when employees from different cultural backgrounds interpret messages differently. Training programs that enhance cross-cultural communication skills are vital in mitigating such issues, ensuring that all team members can collaborate effectively.

Cultural diversity also affects attitudes towards risk and uncertainty. Cultures with high uncertainty avoidance, such as Greece and Portugal, may prefer detailed planning and risk mitigation strategies, while cultures with low uncertainty avoidance, like Singapore and Denmark, may be more comfortable with ambiguity and flexibility. Understanding these tendencies helps organizations tailor their strategic approaches to align with the cultural preferences of their global workforce.

Motivational factors can differ widely across cultures. In individualistic cultures, such as the United States and Australia, personal achievements and autonomy are highly valued, whereas collectivist cultures, like those in many Latin American and African countries, prioritize group harmony and collective success. Effective leaders in global organizations recognize these motivational drivers and adapt their management practices to meet the diverse needs of their employees.

Implementing culturally diverse teams can lead to enhanced creativity and innovation. Different cultural perspectives can inspire novel solutions and approaches to business challenges. However, this diversity also requires adept management to navigate potential conflicts and ensure that all voices are heard. Building a culture of mutual respect and understanding is crucial for harnessing the full potential of a diverse workforce.

Organizations must also be mindful of cultural differences in work-life balance and employee expectations. In some cultures, long working hours and a strong work ethic are the norm, while in others, greater emphasis is placed on leisure time and family commitments. Policies that accommodate these differences can improve employee satisfaction and retention, contributing to overall organizational success.

Leadership in global organizations demands cultural competence. Leaders must be aware of their own cultural biases and strive to understand the cultural backgrounds of their team members. By fostering an inclusive culture that values diversity, leaders can create an environment where all employees feel valued and empowered to contribute their best.

Cultural diversity in global organizations is not merely a challenge to be managed but a strategic asset that can drive innovation, agility, and competitive advantage. By embracing and integrating diverse cultural perspectives, organizations can execute their strategies more effectively and thrive in the global marketplace.

Managing Cross-Cultural Teams

In the ever-evolving landscape of global commerce, the ability to manage cross-cultural teams effectively is paramount. The interaction of diverse cultural backgrounds within a team can introduce a wealth of perspectives, fostering innovation and creativity. However, it can also present unique challenges that require astute management to ensure seamless execution of business strategies.

Understanding the cultural dimensions that influence team dynamics is crucial. Different cultures have varying attitudes towards hierarchy, communication styles, and decision-making processes. For instance, in some cultures, hierarchy is deeply respected, and decisions are typically made by senior leaders. In contrast, other cultures may value egalitarianism and encourage input from all team members. Recognizing these differences can help managers tailor their approach to suit the cultural context of their team members.

Effective communication is the cornerstone of managing cross-cultural teams. Misunderstandings can easily arise from language barriers, differing communication styles, and non-verbal cues. Managers must strive to foster an environment where open and clear communication is encouraged. This can involve setting ground rules for communication, such as encouraging the use of simple language, avoiding idioms, and being mindful of different time zones when scheduling meetings. Additionally, employing active listening techniques can help ensure that all team members feel heard and understood.

Building trust within a cross-cultural team is another critical aspect. Trust can be influenced by cultural norms and previous experiences. In some cultures, trust is built through personal relationships and social interactions, while in others, it may be established through demonstrated competence and reliability. Managers can facilitate trust-building by promoting inclusivity, showing respect for cultural differences, and providing opportunities for team members to connect on a personal level.

Conflict resolution in a cross-cultural context requires sensitivity and a deep understanding of the cultural factors at play. Managers should be equipped with strategies to address conflicts that may arise from cultural misunderstandings. This might involve mediating discussions to ensure that all perspectives are considered and finding common ground that respects the cultural values of all parties involved. Providing training on cultural awareness and conflict resolution can also equip team members with the skills to navigate these challenges effectively.

Leveraging the strengths of a diverse team involves recognizing and valuing the unique contributions that each member brings to the table. This can be achieved by creating an inclusive environment where diverse viewpoints are not only welcomed but actively sought out. Managers should encourage collaboration and knowledge sharing, allowing team members to learn from each other's experiences and expertise. This can lead to more innovative solutions and a more resilient team overall.

Adapting leadership styles to fit the cultural context of the team is essential for effective management. A flexible leadership approach that can shift between directive and participative styles, depending on the cultural expectations of the team, can enhance team cohesion and performance. Managers should be aware of their own cultural biases and strive to lead in a way that is respectful and inclusive of all team members.

In conclusion, managing cross-cultural teams requires a nuanced understanding of cultural differences and a commitment to fostering an inclusive and communicative environment. By prioritizing effective communication, trust-building, conflict resolution, and leveraging the strengths of a diverse team, managers can navigate the complexities of cross-cultural collaboration and drive successful strategy execution.

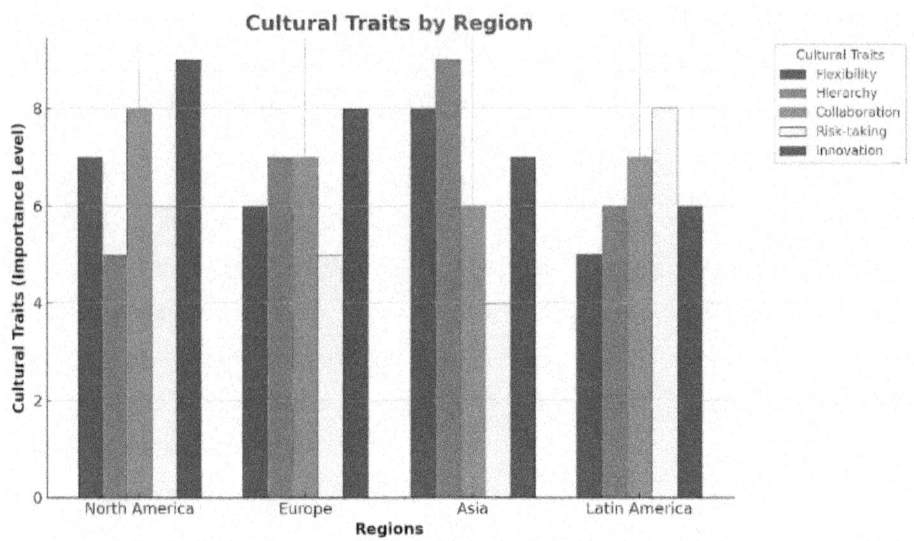

Adapting Culture for Global Strategy Execution

As businesses expand their operations across borders, the importance of aligning corporate culture with global strategy execution becomes paramount. This alignment is not just about understanding different cultures but also about integrating these cultural nuances into the overarching business strategy to ensure seamless operations and cohesive brand identity worldwide. The process involves recognizing the distinct cultural traits that influence business practices in various regions and adapting the corporate culture to accommodate these differences without losing the core values that define the organization.

One of the primary challenges in adapting culture for global strategy execution is the diversity of cultural norms and business etiquettes. For instance, the hierarchical nature of business practices in countries like Japan contrasts sharply with the more egalitarian approach seen in Scandinavian countries. To navigate these differences, companies must develop a nuanced understanding of local customs and integrate these insights into their global strategy. This could mean modifying communication styles, decision-making processes, and leadership approaches to align with local expectations while maintaining the strategic objectives of the company.

Effective communication is a cornerstone of successful global strategy execution. This involves not only language translation but also cultural translation, where the intent and nuances of corporate messages are preserved across different cultural contexts. Multinational companies often employ cultural liaisons or local experts who can bridge the gap between the corporate headquarters and regional offices, ensuring that the strategic vision and corporate values are clearly understood and appropriately implemented.

Moreover, fostering a culturally adaptive leadership team is crucial. Leaders who are culturally intelligent can navigate the complexities of global markets more effectively. They are adept at recognizing cultural differences and leveraging these differences to create competitive advantages. For example, a culturally adaptive leader might recognize that innovation is highly valued in Western markets, while relationship-building and trust are paramount in many Asian markets. By tailoring strategies to these cultural priorities, leaders can drive better engagement and performance across diverse regions.

Training and development programs play a significant role in equipping employees with the skills needed to operate in a global environment. Such programs often include cultural sensitivity training, language courses, and international assignments that expose employees to different cultural settings. These experiences help build a workforce that is not only aware of but also proficient in navigating cultural differences, thereby enhancing the execution of global strategies.

Additionally, the role of technology in bridging cultural gaps cannot be overlooked. Digital tools and platforms enable real-time communication and collaboration across geographies, facilitating the implementation of global strategies. However, companies must be mindful of digital literacy rates and access to technology in different regions to ensure that technological solutions are inclusive and effective.

Adapting corporate culture for global strategy execution also involves aligning incentive and reward systems with cultural expectations. What motivates employees in one culture may not have the same effect in another. For instance, while individual achievements might be celebrated in the United States, collective accomplishments might be more highly valued in countries like Japan. Tailoring reward systems to reflect these cultural preferences can drive higher levels of motivation and performance.

In essence, the adaptation of culture for global strategy execution is a dynamic and ongoing process. It requires a deep understanding of cultural nuances, a commitment to cultural intelligence, and the flexibility to integrate these insights into the corporate fabric. By doing so, companies can not only achieve their strategic goals but also foster a more inclusive and cohesive global workforce.

Global Case Studies

Examining various global businesses reveals the intricate relationship between culture and strategy execution. Each company's unique cultural backdrop significantly influences how strategies are implemented and sustained, showcasing diverse approaches to achieving organizational objectives.

In Japan, Toyota exemplifies a culture deeply rooted in continuous improvement, known as Kaizen. This philosophy permeates every level of the organization, fostering a relentless focus on incremental enhancements and efficiency. Employees are encouraged to identify areas for improvement and suggest solutions, creating a dynamic environment where innovation is a collective responsibility. This cultural foundation has enabled Toyota to maintain its competitive edge and adapt swiftly to changing market demands.

Across the globe in the United States, Google illustrates a distinct approach with its emphasis on a culture of innovation and psychological safety. Google's work environment is designed to promote creativity and risk-taking, allowing employees to experiment without fear of failure. The company's strategy execution thrives on this cultural bedrock, as team members feel empowered to propose groundbreaking ideas and challenge the status quo. This cultural alignment with strategic goals has positioned Google as a leader in technological advancements and market disruption.

In contrast, Germany's Siemens AG showcases a culture characterized by precision, discipline, and engineering excellence. Siemens' strategic execution is deeply tied to its cultural values of meticulous planning and rigorous quality standards. The company's structured approach ensures that strategies are executed with a high degree of accuracy and reliability, reinforcing its reputation for delivering complex engineering projects. Siemens' culture of precision not only drives operational efficiency but also fosters trust and long-term relationships with clients.

India's Tata Group provides another perspective, where a culture of ethical leadership and social responsibility plays a pivotal role in strategy execution. Tata's commitment to integrity and community welfare is embedded in its corporate ethos, influencing strategic decisions and actions. This cultural orientation towards ethical practices and social impact has enabled Tata to build a strong brand reputation and foster loyalty among stakeholders. The alignment of strategic initiatives with cultural values of social good has been instrumental in Tata's sustained success across diverse industries.

In Scandinavia, IKEA's culture of simplicity and sustainability shapes its strategic execution. The company's ethos of cost-consciousness and environmental stewardship is reflected in its strategy to provide affordable, eco-friendly products. IKEA's culture encourages employees to find innovative ways to reduce costs and minimize environmental impact, aligning with its strategic objectives. This cultural commitment to simplicity and sustainability has allowed IKEA to expand globally while maintaining its core values and customer appeal.

A closer look at Brazil's Natura & Co reveals a culture that prioritizes relationships and inclusivity. Natura's strategy execution benefits from a collaborative work environment where diverse perspectives are valued. This inclusive culture fosters a sense of belonging and mutual respect, driving employee engagement and innovation. Natura's strategic initiatives in sustainability and social responsibility are seamlessly integrated with its cultural focus on relationships, enhancing its brand image and market position.

These global case studies illustrate that the interplay between culture and strategy execution is multifaceted and context-specific. Each company's cultural attributes significantly shape how strategies are developed, communicated, and implemented. Understanding and leveraging cultural strengths can lead to more effective strategy execution, ultimately driving organizational success in a competitive global landscape.

Chapter 09

Sustaining a High-Performance Culture

Key Elements of a High-Performance Culture

A high-performance culture is the bedrock upon which successful strategy execution is built. It is characterized by several fundamental elements that collectively create an environment where individuals and teams can excel, innovate, and drive the organization towards its strategic goals. At its core, a high-performance culture is distinguished by clear and compelling vision and values that are consistently communicated and modeled by leadership. This vision serves as a guiding star, aligning the efforts of all employees and providing a sense of purpose and direction.

One of the primary elements of a high-performance culture is a strong emphasis on accountability. In such an environment, individuals are not only aware of their responsibilities but are also held accountable for their actions and outcomes. This accountability is fostered through transparent performance metrics, regular feedback, and a robust system of rewards and consequences. Employees understand that their contributions are critical to the organization's success, and they are motivated to perform at their best.

Another key element is a commitment to continuous learning and improvement. Organizations with high-performance cultures invest in the development of their employees, providing opportunities for training, skill enhancement, and career growth. This commitment extends beyond formal training programs to include a culture of knowledge sharing, where employees are encouraged to share their expertise and learn from one another. This focus on learning not only enhances individual capabilities but also drives innovation and adaptability within the organization.

Effective communication is also a hallmark of a high-performance culture. Open, honest, and transparent communication channels ensure that information flows freely across all levels of the organization. Leaders are approachable and actively listen to their employees, fostering a sense of trust and collaboration. This open communication helps to break down silos, align efforts, and ensure that everyone is working towards common goals.

Empowerment and autonomy are equally crucial in a high-performance culture. Employees are given the authority and resources they need to make decisions and take ownership of their work. This empowerment fosters a sense of responsibility and pride, as individuals feel that their contributions are valued and that they have the ability to make a meaningful impact. Autonomy also encourages creativity and innovation, as employees are free to explore new ideas and approaches without being stifled by rigid hierarchies or micromanagement.

Recognition and reward systems play a significant role in reinforcing a high-performance culture. Organizations that excel in strategy execution understand the importance of celebrating successes and acknowledging the efforts of their employees. Recognition can take many forms, from formal awards and bonuses to informal praise and appreciation. These gestures not only boost morale but also reinforce the behaviors and attitudes that contribute to high performance.

Lastly, a high-performance culture is underpinned by a strong sense of teamwork and collaboration. Employees work together towards shared goals, leveraging each other's strengths and supporting one another in overcoming challenges. This collaborative spirit is cultivated through team-building activities, cross-functional projects, and a general ethos of mutual respect and support.

In essence, the key elements of a high-performance culture—clear vision and values, accountability, continuous learning, effective communication, empowerment, recognition, and teamwork—create an environment where strategy execution can thrive. These elements are interrelated and mutually reinforcing, each contributing to a culture that drives organizational success.

Indicator of High-Performance Culture	Corresponding Metric
Employee Engagement	Employee Retention Rate
Innovation Rate	Number of New Products Launched
Customer Satisfaction	Net Promoter Score (NPS)
Operational Efficiency	Time to Market
Leadership Effectiveness	360-Degree Leadership Feedback Scores
Collaboration	Number of Cross-functional Projects Completed

Leadership's Role in Sustaining Performance

Leaders play a pivotal role in maintaining and enhancing performance within an organization. Their influence is not merely confined to setting strategic directions but extends deeply into the cultural fabric of the company. A leader's actions, decisions, and behaviors significantly shape the organizational environment, creating a context where strategy can be effectively executed.

At the heart of sustaining performance is the leader's ability to cultivate a culture of accountability and continuous improvement. This involves setting clear expectations and providing the necessary resources for employees to meet those expectations. Leaders must foster an environment where feedback is not only welcomed but actively sought. This open communication channel encourages employees to share insights and ideas, facilitating a culture of collaboration and innovation.

Moreover, leaders must demonstrate a commitment to the organization's values and mission. Their behavior sets a benchmark for others to follow. When leaders consistently align their actions with the company's core values, it reinforces those values throughout the organization. This alignment helps in creating a unified direction and purpose, which is crucial for sustained performance.

Effective leaders also recognize the importance of developing their team. They invest in training and development programs, ensuring that employees have the skills and knowledge necessary to excel in their roles. By promoting a learning culture, leaders not only enhance individual capabilities but also drive organizational growth. This commitment to development signals to employees that the organization values their growth, thereby increasing engagement and retention.

Recognition and reward systems are another critical aspect of sustaining performance. Leaders must ensure that these systems are fair and transparent, recognizing not just the outcomes but also the efforts and behaviors that contribute to those outcomes. When employees feel that their contributions are acknowledged and valued, their motivation to perform is significantly enhanced.

Adaptability is a key trait for leaders in sustaining performance. The business environment is dynamic, and leaders must be able to navigate through changes effectively. This requires a proactive approach to identifying potential challenges and opportunities and being prepared to pivot strategies as needed. Leaders who can manage change effectively help their organizations remain resilient and competitive.

In addition, leaders must foster a sense of ownership among employees. When individuals feel a sense of ownership over their work, they are more likely to take initiative and go above and beyond in their roles. This sense of ownership is cultivated through trust and empowerment. Leaders must delegate responsibilities and trust their teams to make decisions. This empowerment not only boosts morale but also drives performance as employees feel more connected to the organization's success.

Leaders also need to be role models of ethical behavior. Ethical leadership builds trust and credibility, both within the organization and with external stakeholders. When leaders act with integrity and fairness, it sets a standard for the entire organization, promoting a culture of ethical behavior that supports long-term performance.

In essence, the role of leadership in sustaining performance is multifaceted, encompassing the establishment of a supportive culture, commitment to development, recognition of contributions, adaptability, empowerment, and ethical behavior. Leaders who excel in these areas create an environment where strategy can be effectively executed, driving sustained performance and organizational success.

Maintaining Employee Engagement and Motivation

In the landscape of modern business, the vitality of an organization often hinges on its ability to keep employees engaged and motivated. This dynamic interplay between engagement and motivation is not merely a byproduct of good management; it is a strategic imperative that fuels productivity, fosters innovation, and sustains competitive advantage. To cultivate an environment where employees feel genuinely connected to their work, leaders must adopt a multifaceted approach that transcends traditional incentives and delves into the psychological and emotional drivers of human behavior.

Creating a workplace culture that prioritizes engagement begins with a clear and compelling vision. Employees need to understand not just what they are doing, but why they are doing it. This sense of purpose can be a powerful motivator, aligning individual goals with the broader objectives of the organization. When employees see how their contributions make a tangible difference, their commitment to their roles and responsibilities deepens. Leaders must communicate this vision consistently and authentically, ensuring that it resonates at all levels of the organization.

Autonomy is another critical factor in maintaining high levels of engagement. Empowering employees to take ownership of their tasks and make decisions fosters a sense of responsibility and pride in their work. This autonomy should be balanced with adequate support and resources, enabling employees to perform their duties effectively without feeling overwhelmed. By entrusting employees with meaningful responsibilities and recognizing their expertise, organizations can cultivate a culture of trust and respect.

Recognition and rewards also play a pivotal role in sustaining motivation. While financial incentives are important, they are not the sole drivers of engagement. Regular, genuine recognition of employees' efforts and achievements can have a profound impact on their morale. This recognition should be timely and specific, highlighting the behaviors and outcomes that align with the organization's values and goals. Celebrating successes, both big and small, reinforces a positive work environment and encourages continued excellence.

Opportunities for growth and development are equally essential in maintaining engagement. Employees who perceive a clear path for advancement within the organization are more likely to invest in their roles and strive for higher performance. Professional development programs, mentorship opportunities, and ongoing training can help employees acquire new skills and advance their careers. By supporting continuous learning and development, organizations demonstrate their commitment to their employees' long-term success.

Work-life balance is another crucial element in fostering a motivated workforce. In today's fast-paced business environment, the lines between work and personal life can often blur, leading to burnout and disengagement. Organizations must prioritize the well-being of their employees by promoting flexible work arrangements, encouraging regular breaks, and providing access to wellness programs. A healthy work-life balance not only enhances employee satisfaction but also boosts productivity and retention.

Effective communication is the glue that binds these elements together. Transparent, open communication channels ensure that employees feel heard and valued. Regular feedback, both positive and constructive, helps employees understand their strengths and areas for improvement. Leaders should also be approachable and accessible, fostering an environment where employees feel comfortable sharing their ideas and concerns.

By integrating these strategies into the fabric of the organizational culture, businesses can create a thriving, engaged workforce that is motivated to achieve exceptional results. Employee engagement and motivation are not static; they require ongoing attention and adaptation to meet the evolving needs of the workforce. Through deliberate and thoughtful actions, leaders can inspire their teams to reach new heights, driving the organization towards sustained success.

Long-Term Strategies for Sustained Performance

Achieving sustained performance in a business environment often requires a commitment to long-term strategies that align closely with the organization's culture. One of the foundational elements is the development of a vision that extends beyond immediate gains and short-term metrics. This vision should be communicated clearly and consistently across all levels of the organization, ensuring that every team member understands their role in the broader picture. A shared vision fosters a sense of purpose and drives collective efforts towards common goals.

Another critical component is the establishment of robust governance structures. These structures should be designed to support strategic objectives while maintaining flexibility to adapt to changing market conditions. Effective governance involves setting clear policies, procedures, and accountability mechanisms that guide decision-making processes. It is important that these structures are not overly rigid, as they must allow for innovation and responsiveness.

Investment in human capital is also paramount. Organizations that prioritize continuous learning and development are better equipped to adapt to evolving business landscapes. This involves not only formal training programs but also creating an environment that encourages knowledge sharing and mentorship. By cultivating a culture of continuous improvement, companies can ensure that their workforce remains agile and capable of meeting future challenges.

Strategic partnerships and alliances can play a significant role in sustaining performance over the long term. Collaborating with other organizations can provide access to new markets, technologies, and expertise. These partnerships should be strategic and aligned with the company's core values and long-term objectives. It is essential to manage these relationships carefully, with clear agreements and mutual benefits, to ensure they contribute positively to sustained performance.

Resource allocation is another critical area. Long-term strategies require a thoughtful approach to allocating financial, human, and technological resources. It is crucial to strike a balance between investing in current operations and funding future initiatives. This often involves difficult decisions about where to cut costs and where to invest more heavily. Effective resource management ensures that the organization can sustain its performance without compromising on quality or innovation.

The role of leadership in driving long-term strategies cannot be overstated. Leaders must be visionary and capable of inspiring their teams to commit to long-term goals. They should model the values and behaviors that are expected within the organization, fostering a culture of integrity and accountability. Effective leaders are also adept at navigating the complexities of change management, guiding their teams through transitions smoothly and maintaining focus on strategic objectives.

Technology and data analytics are increasingly important in supporting long-term strategies. Leveraging advanced technologies can enhance operational efficiencies, improve customer experiences, and provide insights that inform strategic decisions. Data analytics, in particular, allows organizations to track performance metrics, identify trends, and make data-driven decisions. By integrating technology into their strategic planning, companies can remain competitive and agile.

Sustained performance also hinges on the organization's ability to innovate. This involves fostering a culture that encourages creativity and experimentation. Organizations should provide the resources and support necessary for innovation to thrive, including dedicated time for research and development, and a safe environment for taking calculated risks. By embedding innovation into the core of their operations, companies can continuously evolve and stay ahead of industry trends.

In essence, long-term strategies for sustained performance require a holistic approach that integrates vision, governance, human capital, partnerships, resource management, leadership, technology, and innovation. Each of these elements must be aligned with the organization's culture and strategic objectives, creating a cohesive and resilient framework that supports ongoing success.

Chapter 10

The Role of Technology in Shaping Culture

Digital Transformation and Culture

The rapid advancement of technology has fundamentally altered the landscape of business operations and strategy execution. Digital transformation is not merely an operational upgrade; it represents a profound shift that affects all aspects of an organization. This transformation necessitates a reevaluation of existing business models, processes, and, crucially, the underlying culture that supports them. For organizations to thrive in this digital age, a cohesive and adaptive culture becomes indispensable.

At the heart of digital transformation lies the integration of digital technology into all areas of a business, resulting in significant changes in how companies operate and deliver value to customers. This integration goes beyond the implementation of new software or hardware; it involves rethinking the way businesses interact with their environment and stakeholders. The cultural aspect of this shift is often the most challenging yet the most critical component to address.

A digital culture cultivates an environment where continuous learning, agility, and innovation are not just encouraged but are foundational principles. Employees at all levels need to be empowered to think creatively, take calculated risks, and embrace new ideas without fear of failure. This cultural shift requires strong leadership committed to fostering an atmosphere of trust and open communication. Leaders must model the behaviors they wish to see, demonstrating a willingness to adapt and learn alongside their teams.

One of the main barriers to digital transformation is resistance to change. Employees accustomed to traditional ways of working may feel threatened or unsure about new technologies and processes. Overcoming this resistance involves more than just training sessions and workshops; it requires a deep-seated cultural change. Organizations must create a narrative that connects the digital transformation to the company's core values and mission. By doing so, employees can see the transformation not as a disruptive force but as an evolution that aligns with the company's long-term vision.

Another significant aspect of a digital culture is the emphasis on data-driven decision-making. In a digitally transformed organization, decisions are increasingly based on data analytics and insights rather than intuition or experience alone. This shift necessitates a culture that values transparency, where data is accessible, and employees are trained to interpret and utilize this information effectively. The democratization of data empowers employees to make informed decisions, fostering a sense of ownership and accountability.

Collaboration also takes on a new dimension in a digital culture. The traditional hierarchical structures often give way to more fluid, cross-functional teams that can respond swiftly to changes in the market or technology landscape. These teams leverage digital tools to enhance communication, streamline workflows, and drive innovation. The cultural shift towards collaboration ensures that knowledge and expertise are shared across the organization, breaking down silos and fostering a more inclusive environment.

The role of continuous improvement cannot be overstated in a digital culture. The rapid pace of technological change means that organizations must be in a constant state of evolution. This requires a culture that not only accepts but anticipates change. Regular feedback loops, iterative processes, and a focus on incremental improvements help organizations stay ahead of the curve.

Ultimately, the success of digital transformation is inextricably linked to the culture that supports it. A digital culture is one that is resilient, adaptable, and forward-thinking. It is a culture that not only accepts change but thrives on it, viewing each challenge as an opportunity for growth and innovation. For businesses aiming to execute their strategies effectively in the digital age, cultivating such a culture is not optional but essential.

Technology-Driven Cultural Change

The rapid advancement of technology has significantly altered the landscape of business culture, shaping how organizations execute their strategies. With the integration of digital tools and platforms, companies can now streamline processes, enhance communication, and foster innovation in ways that were previously unimaginable. This transformation is not merely about adopting new gadgets or software; it fundamentally changes the way businesses operate, interact, and compete in the market.

At the core of this transformation is the rise of data analytics. Businesses now have access to vast amounts of data, providing insights that drive decision-making. This data-centric approach allows for more precise targeting of customer needs, optimizing operations, and predicting market trends. The ability to analyze and interpret data effectively becomes a crucial skill within corporate culture, encouraging a shift towards evidence-based strategies over intuition or tradition.

Another significant impact of technology on business culture is the evolution of communication. With the advent of instant messaging, video conferencing, and collaborative platforms, geographical barriers are virtually eliminated. Teams can work together seamlessly from different parts of the world, fostering a more inclusive and diverse work environment. This connectivity enhances teamwork and ensures that information flows freely across all levels of an organization, breaking down silos that traditionally hindered progress.

Automation and artificial intelligence (AI) are also redefining roles and responsibilities within companies. Routine tasks that once required significant human effort can now be automated, allowing employees to focus on more strategic and creative endeavors. This shift not only increases efficiency but also requires a cultural adaptation where continuous learning and flexibility are paramount. Employees must be willing to adapt to new tools and workflows, fostering a culture of innovation and resilience.

The integration of technology into business processes also necessitates a change in leadership styles. Leaders must now be tech-savvy and capable of navigating the complexities of a digital world. This includes understanding the implications of cybersecurity, data privacy, and digital ethics. Leaders are expected to foster an environment where technological adoption is encouraged and supported, ensuring that their teams are equipped with the necessary skills and resources to thrive.

Moreover, the rise of remote work, accelerated by technological advancements, requires a rethinking of workplace culture. Organizations must create virtual environments that maintain engagement, productivity, and a sense of community. This includes developing new norms and practices for remote collaboration, performance evaluation, and employee well-being. Technology enables flexibility, but it also demands a deliberate effort to sustain a cohesive and motivated workforce.

Consumer expectations have also evolved with technology. Customers now expect seamless digital experiences, personalized interactions, and instant gratification. Businesses must adapt their strategies to meet these demands, leveraging technology to enhance customer service and engagement. This shift towards a customer-centric approach requires a cultural alignment where every employee understands and values the importance of customer satisfaction.

In this era of rapid technological change, businesses must cultivate a culture that is agile, innovative, and data-driven. Embracing technology is not just about staying competitive; it is about creating a resilient and forward-thinking organization capable of navigating the uncertainties of the future. As technology continues to evolve, so too must the cultural frameworks that support strategic execution, ensuring that organizations remain adaptable and poised for success in an increasingly digital world.

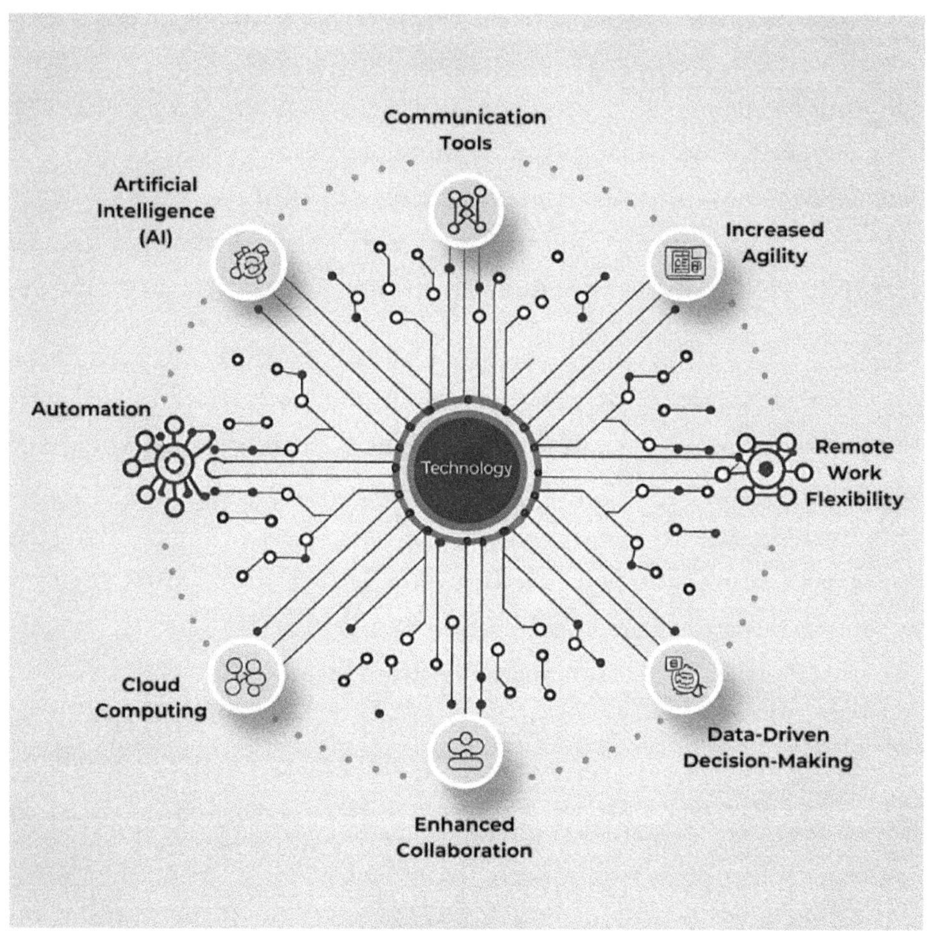

Leveraging Technology for Strategy Execution

In the modern business landscape, technology stands as a pivotal force, reshaping how organizations execute their strategies. The integration of advanced technological tools and systems into business operations is no longer a luxury but a necessity for achieving strategic goals. Companies that effectively leverage technology can streamline processes, enhance decision-making, and foster a culture of innovation, all of which are critical for successful strategy execution.

The first aspect to consider is the role of data analytics. By harnessing the power of big data, businesses can gain valuable insights into market trends, customer behaviors, and operational efficiencies. Data analytics enables decision-makers to make informed choices, reducing uncertainty and aligning actions with strategic objectives. Predictive analytics, in particular, can forecast future trends, allowing companies to anticipate changes and adapt their strategies proactively.

Another crucial element is the implementation of enterprise resource planning (ERP) systems. These systems integrate various business processes, from finance and human resources to supply chain management and customer relations. By providing a unified platform, ERP systems ensure that information flows seamlessly across departments, enhancing coordination and reducing redundancies. This integration is vital for maintaining alignment between different parts of the organization and ensuring that everyone is working towards the same strategic goals.

Customer relationship management (CRM) systems also play a significant role in strategy execution. By centralizing customer data, CRM systems enable businesses to deliver personalized experiences, improve customer satisfaction, and build long-term loyalty. Understanding customer needs and preferences allows companies to tailor their offerings and marketing efforts, ensuring that they resonate with the target audience. This alignment with customer expectations is crucial for achieving strategic marketing and sales objectives.

The rise of artificial intelligence (AI) and machine learning (ML) has further transformed the strategic landscape. These technologies can automate routine tasks, freeing up human resources for more complex and strategic activities. AI-driven insights can identify patterns and trends that might be overlooked by human analysts, providing a competitive edge. For instance, AI can optimize supply chain operations by predicting demand fluctuations and adjusting inventory levels accordingly, thus supporting strategic goals related to efficiency and cost reduction.

Cloud computing is another technological advancement that supports strategy execution. By offering scalable and flexible IT resources, cloud computing allows businesses to rapidly deploy new applications and services. This agility is essential in a fast-paced business environment where the ability to quickly respond to market changes can be a significant strategic advantage. Moreover, cloud-based collaboration tools facilitate communication and teamwork, ensuring that all stakeholders are aligned and informed.

Cybersecurity is an often-overlooked but critical component of leveraging technology for strategy execution. Protecting sensitive data and ensuring the integrity of information systems is paramount for maintaining trust and operational continuity. A robust cybersecurity strategy safeguards against threats that could derail strategic initiatives and cause significant financial and reputational damage.

The integration of technology into business processes must be supported by a culture that embraces innovation and continuous improvement. This requires leadership that champions technological adoption and invests in training and development to equip employees with the necessary skills. A culture that encourages experimentation and learning from failures can drive technological advancements and strategic success.

In essence, technology acts as an enabler, providing the tools and platforms necessary for executing business strategies effectively.

By leveraging data analytics, ERP systems, CRM systems, AI, cloud computing, and cybersecurity measures, businesses can enhance their operational efficiency, make informed decisions, and stay ahead in a competitive market. The synergy between technology and strategy execution is undeniable, and organizations that master this relationship are well-positioned for long-term success.

Case Studies of Technological Impact on Culture

Technological advancements have profoundly influenced business culture, shaping strategies and execution in ways previously unimaginable. To illustrate this dynamic interaction, various case studies offer a window into how organizations have navigated these changes and the resulting impacts on their cultural landscapes.

One prominent example is the transformation at General Electric (GE) under the leadership of Jack Welch in the late 20th century. GE's immersion into digital technologies catalyzed a shift towards a more agile and responsive corporate culture. Welch's implementation of Six Sigma, a data-driven management approach, exemplified the fusion of technology and culture. By embedding Six Sigma into the company's DNA, GE not only improved operational efficiency but also fostered a culture of continuous improvement and accountability. This case underscores how technology can serve as a lever for cultural change, driving a commitment to excellence and precision across an organization.

The retail giant Walmart offers another compelling case. With the advent of sophisticated data analytics and supply chain technologies, Walmart revolutionized its inventory management and customer service. The integration of these technologies necessitated a cultural shift towards data-centric decision-making. Employees at all levels were trained to interpret data and leverage insights to enhance customer satisfaction and operational efficiency. This cultural shift was instrumental in maintaining Walmart's competitive edge, demonstrating how technology can reorient a company's cultural focus towards innovation and customer-centricity.

Netflix's evolution from a DVD rental service to a streaming behemoth provides a vivid example of how technological disruption can redefine a company's culture. The shift to streaming required Netflix to cultivate a culture of agility and innovation. The company adopted a Silicon Valley mindset, characterized by risk-taking, experimentation, and a tolerance for failure. This cultural transformation was crucial for Netflix to stay ahead in the rapidly changing entertainment industry. By embracing technology, Netflix not only transformed its business model but also fostered a culture that thrives on constant innovation and adaptation.

In the financial sector, Goldman Sachs provides insight into how technology can reshape organizational culture. As financial markets became increasingly complex and data-driven, Goldman Sachs invested heavily in technology to maintain its competitive advantage. The firm integrated advanced algorithms and artificial intelligence into its trading operations, which required a cultural shift towards a more collaborative and interdisciplinary approach. Technologists and traders began working closely together, breaking down traditional silos and fostering a culture of cross-functional collaboration. This case highlights the role of technology in dismantling cultural barriers and promoting a more integrated and cohesive organizational environment.

The healthcare industry, too, has witnessed significant cultural transformations driven by technology. Mayo Clinic's adoption of electronic health records (EHRs) is a prime example. The implementation of EHRs required a substantial cultural shift from paper-based to digital workflows. This transition not only improved patient care and operational efficiency but also necessitated a culture of continuous learning and adaptation among healthcare professionals. Training programs and support systems were established to help staff navigate the new digital landscape, fostering a culture of technological proficiency and patient-centric care.

These case studies underscore the profound impact of technology on business culture. They reveal how technological advancements can serve as catalysts for cultural change, driving organizations towards greater efficiency, innovation, and customer focus. By examining these examples, it becomes evident that the interplay between technology and culture is pivotal for successful strategy execution. Organizations that effectively integrate technology into their cultural fabric are better positioned to navigate the complexities of the modern business environment and achieve sustained success.

Chapter 11

Ethical Considerations in Business Culture

Defining Ethical Business Culture

Ethical business culture forms the bedrock of any successful organization, blending core values with daily practices to create an environment where integrity thrives. This subchapter delves into the essence of what constitutes an ethical business culture, examining its critical components and the role it plays in driving strategy execution.

At its heart, an ethical business culture is defined by a set of shared values and principles that guide the behavior of all members within the organization. These values often include honesty, transparency, fairness, and respect, which collectively foster an atmosphere of trust and collaboration. When these principles are deeply ingrained in the corporate DNA, they shape decision-making processes, influence interactions among employees, and impact relationships with external stakeholders.

One of the primary characteristics of an ethical business culture is the presence of a well-defined code of ethics. This code serves as a formal document that outlines the expected standards of conduct and provides a framework for ethical decision-making. It is not merely a set of rules, but a reflection of the organization's commitment to uphold high moral standards. Employees at all levels are encouraged to internalize and adhere to these guidelines, ensuring consistency and accountability across the board.

Leadership plays a pivotal role in cultivating and maintaining an ethical business culture. Leaders who demonstrate ethical behavior set a powerful example for their teams, reinforcing the importance of integrity in every action and decision. They are responsible for creating an environment where ethical conduct is recognized and rewarded, and where unethical behavior is promptly addressed. By embodying the values they wish to see, leaders can inspire their employees to follow suit, thereby embedding ethical practices into the organizational fabric.

Communication is another crucial element in defining ethical business culture. Open and honest communication channels allow for the free flow of information, enabling employees to voice concerns, report unethical behavior, and seek guidance without fear of retaliation. Regular training sessions and workshops on ethics can further reinforce the organization's commitment to ethical standards, providing employees with the tools and knowledge they need to navigate complex ethical dilemmas.

An ethical business culture also emphasizes the importance of corporate social responsibility (CSR). Organizations that prioritize CSR initiatives demonstrate their commitment to making a positive impact on society and the environment. This not only enhances the company's reputation but also aligns its operations with broader societal values, fostering goodwill and trust among consumers and stakeholders. Ethical practices in areas such as environmental sustainability, fair labor practices, and community engagement are integral to building a culture that values more than just profit.

Moreover, ethical business culture is not static; it evolves with the organization and the external environment. Continuous evaluation and improvement are necessary to ensure that the culture remains relevant and effective. Regular assessments, feedback mechanisms, and ethical audits can help identify areas for improvement and reinforce the organization's dedication to ethical excellence.

In essence, defining ethical business culture involves more than just establishing a set of rules; it requires a holistic approach that integrates ethical values into every aspect of the organization. By fostering a culture where integrity is paramount, organizations can create a solid foundation for executing their strategic objectives effectively and sustainably.

Embedding Ethics into Organizational Culture

Within the intricate tapestry of organizational culture, the infusion of ethics stands as a cornerstone. This integration is not merely an afterthought or a checkbox exercise. It is a deliberate, thoughtful process that permeates every facet of a business, shaping its core values, guiding principles, and daily operations.

At the heart of embedding ethics into organizational culture lies a deep commitment from leadership. Leaders set the tone for ethical behavior through their actions and decisions. They must consistently demonstrate integrity, transparency, and accountability, serving as role models for employees at all levels. This top-down approach ensures that ethical considerations are not sidelined but are integral to the decision-making process.

Training and development programs play a crucial role in fostering an ethical culture. These programs should be designed to educate employees about the importance of ethics in the workplace, providing them with the tools and knowledge to navigate complex situations. Regular workshops, seminars, and e-learning modules can reinforce ethical standards and keep them at the forefront of employees' minds.

Communication is another vital element. Clear, consistent messaging about the organization's ethical expectations helps to build a shared understanding among employees. This can be achieved through various channels, including internal newsletters, emails, and town hall meetings. Open dialogues about ethical dilemmas and challenges encourage a culture of transparency and trust, where employees feel comfortable raising concerns and discussing potential issues.

Policies and procedures must align with ethical standards. Organizations should establish a comprehensive code of ethics that outlines acceptable behaviors and practices. This code should be easily accessible and regularly reviewed to ensure it remains relevant in a changing business environment. Additionally, mechanisms for reporting unethical behavior, such as whistleblower hotlines, should be in place to protect and support those who speak out.

Performance management systems should incorporate ethical behavior as a key criterion. Recognizing and rewarding employees who demonstrate a strong commitment to ethics reinforces the importance of these values. Conversely, there should be clear consequences for unethical behavior, ensuring that there is no ambiguity about the organization's stance on integrity.

The role of corporate social responsibility (CSR) initiatives cannot be overlooked. These initiatives reflect the organization's commitment to ethical practices beyond its immediate business operations. By engaging in activities that benefit society and the environment, organizations can demonstrate their ethical values in action, further embedding these principles into their culture.

Regular audits and assessments help to ensure that ethical standards are being upheld. These evaluations can identify areas for improvement and highlight best practices. By continually monitoring and refining their approach to ethics, organizations can maintain high standards and adapt to new ethical challenges as they arise.

In the broader context, fostering an ethical culture contributes to long-term success. It builds trust with stakeholders, enhances the organization's reputation, and creates a positive work environment. Employees who feel that they are part of an ethical organization are likely to be more engaged, motivated, and loyal.

The integration of ethics into organizational culture is a dynamic, ongoing process. It requires dedication, vigilance, and a proactive approach. By embedding ethical principles deeply within their culture, organizations can navigate the complexities of the business world with integrity and purpose.

Ethics and Strategy Execution

In the realm of business culture, the intersection of ethics and strategy execution is a critical focal point. Ethical considerations are not merely peripheral elements but foundational to the successful implementation of any strategic plan. When organizations align their ethical standards with their strategic objectives, they cultivate an environment where integrity and performance coexist harmoniously.

Ethics serve as the moral compass guiding decision-making processes and actions within a company. This moral framework ensures that strategies are not only effective but also sustainable and socially responsible. An ethical approach to strategy execution demands transparency, accountability, and fairness. These principles foster trust among stakeholders, including employees, customers, investors, and the broader community.

One of the key aspects of integrating ethics into strategy execution is the establishment of a robust ethical framework. This framework should be clearly articulated and communicated throughout the organization. It involves setting clear ethical guidelines and expectations, which are then embedded into the strategic planning and execution processes. Leadership plays a pivotal role in this integration, as leaders must model ethical behavior and reinforce the importance of ethics in achieving strategic goals.

Moreover, ethical considerations must be woven into the fabric of the corporate culture. This involves creating a culture where ethical behavior is recognized and rewarded, and unethical behavior is swiftly addressed. Employees should feel empowered to voice ethical concerns without fear of retaliation. This can be achieved through mechanisms such as anonymous reporting systems and whistleblower protections.

The alignment of ethics with strategy execution also necessitates regular training and education. Continuous learning opportunities help employees understand the ethical dimensions of their roles and the broader implications of their actions. Training programs should cover topics such as ethical decision-making, conflict of interest, and compliance with legal and regulatory requirements. By investing in ethical education, organizations can ensure that their workforce is equipped to navigate complex ethical dilemmas.

In addition to internal measures, organizations must also consider the ethical implications of their external partnerships and supply chains. Ethical strategy execution extends beyond the boundaries of the organization to include the ethical practices of suppliers, contractors, and business partners. Companies should conduct thorough due diligence to ensure that their partners adhere to similar ethical standards. This not only mitigates risks but also reinforces the organization's commitment to ethical conduct.

The impact of ethics on strategy execution is profound. Ethical organizations tend to enjoy higher levels of employee engagement and customer loyalty. When stakeholders trust that a company operates with integrity, they are more likely to support its strategic initiatives. Conversely, ethical breaches can lead to reputational damage, legal consequences, and financial losses, all of which can derail strategic objectives.

In practice, integrating ethics into strategy execution requires a proactive and deliberate approach. It demands that organizations move beyond compliance and embrace a genuine commitment to ethical principles. This commitment should be reflected in every aspect of the organization's operations, from strategic planning to day-to-day decision-making.

Ultimately, the synergy between ethics and strategy execution can drive long-term success and sustainability. By prioritizing ethical considerations, organizations can build a solid foundation for achieving their strategic goals while maintaining the trust and respect of their stakeholders.

Case Studies of Ethical Cultures

The exploration of ethical cultures within various organizations offers a profound understanding of how these cultures can significantly influence business practices and strategy execution. This subchapter delves into specific case studies, shedding light on companies that have successfully integrated ethical principles into their core operations, thereby achieving remarkable strategic outcomes.

One notable example is Company A, a multinational corporation in the technology sector. This company has developed a robust ethical framework that permeates every level of its operations. The company's commitment to transparency and accountability is evident in its comprehensive code of conduct, which is regularly updated to reflect emerging ethical challenges. Employees are encouraged to report unethical behavior through an anonymous hotline, ensuring that concerns can be raised without fear of retaliation. This open environment fosters trust and cooperation, which in turn enhances the company's ability to execute its strategy effectively.

Another compelling case is Company B, a leading firm in the pharmaceutical industry. Company B has made ethical considerations a central component of its business model, particularly in its approach to research and development. The company has implemented stringent ethical guidelines for clinical trials, prioritizing patient safety and informed consent. These guidelines are not merely regulatory compliance measures but are deeply ingrained in the company's culture. By prioritizing ethical practices, Company B has built a reputation for integrity and reliability, which has proven to be a significant competitive advantage in a heavily scrutinized industry.

In the financial sector, Company C provides a striking example of how ethical culture can drive strategic success. After facing a major scandal, Company C undertook a comprehensive overhaul of its corporate governance structures. The introduction of rigorous ethical training programs for all employees, coupled with the establishment of an independent ethics committee, marked a transformative shift in the company's culture. This renewed focus on ethical behavior has restored stakeholder confidence and has been instrumental in the company's recovery and growth.

The retail industry also offers valuable insights, as demonstrated by Company D. This company has embedded ethical sourcing practices into its supply chain management. By committing to fair labor practices and environmental sustainability, Company D has not only mitigated risks associated with unethical suppliers but has also enhanced its brand image. Customers increasingly value ethical considerations, and Company D's transparent supply chain practices have attracted a loyal customer base, driving long-term profitability.

These case studies underscore the critical role of ethical culture in strategy execution. They illustrate that ethical considerations are not merely peripheral concerns but are integral to achieving strategic objectives. Companies that prioritize ethical behavior create environments where employees feel valued and motivated, leading to higher levels of engagement and productivity. Furthermore, these companies build strong relationships with stakeholders, including customers, investors, and regulatory bodies, which are essential for sustained success.

The common thread across these case studies is the deliberate and sustained effort to embed ethical principles into the organizational fabric. Whether through comprehensive codes of conduct, rigorous ethical guidelines, or transparent supply chain practices, these companies demonstrate that ethical culture is a powerful driver of strategic success. By fostering environments where ethical behavior is the norm, they not only navigate complex challenges more effectively but also achieve a competitive edge in their respective industries.

Chapter 12

Measuring the Impact of Culture on Strategy Execution

Key Metrics for Cultural Impact

In the intricate dance of strategy execution, understanding the cultural fabric of an organization is paramount. Cultural impact transcends the superficial, embedding itself in the very essence of how a company operates, innovates, and thrives. To gauge this impact effectively, one must delve into specific metrics that illuminate the nuances of organizational culture. These metrics serve as vital signposts, guiding leaders in nurturing an environment conducive to strategic success.

Employee engagement stands as a cornerstone metric, reflecting the emotional and intellectual commitment of the workforce. High levels of engagement indicate a culture where individuals feel valued, motivated, and aligned with the company's vision. This can be measured through surveys and feedback mechanisms that assess job satisfaction, loyalty, and the willingness to go above and beyond. Engaged employees are often more productive, innovative, and resilient, driving the organization's strategic objectives forward with vigor.

Another critical metric is the rate of employee turnover. High turnover rates can signal underlying cultural issues, such as dissatisfaction, lack of career growth opportunities, or misalignment with the company's values. Conversely, low turnover rates often suggest a stable and positive work environment. Analyzing exit interviews and conducting stay interviews can provide deeper insights into the reasons behind turnover, offering a clearer picture of the cultural landscape.

Diversity and inclusion metrics are also pivotal in assessing cultural impact. A diverse workforce brings a wealth of perspectives and ideas, fostering innovation and problem-solving. Tracking the representation of various demographic groups within the organization, as well as their advancement and retention rates, can highlight the inclusivity of the culture. Furthermore, employee perceptions of inclusivity, gathered through surveys and focus groups, can reveal whether the organization truly embraces diversity or merely pays lip service to it.

The frequency and nature of internal communications offer another window into the cultural milieu. Effective communication channels that encourage transparency, openness, and collaboration are indicative of a healthy culture. Metrics such as the number of town hall meetings, the use of collaborative tools, and the frequency of cross-departmental projects can shed light on the organization's communication practices. Additionally, the responsiveness and engagement levels in these communications can further illustrate the organization's commitment to fostering a connected and informed workforce.

Innovation metrics, such as the number of new ideas generated, patents filed, or product launches, can also serve as cultural indicators. A culture that encourages experimentation, risk-taking, and creative thinking is likely to excel in innovation. Employee participation in idea generation programs, hackathons, and innovation challenges can be tracked to gauge the vibrancy of the innovative spirit within the organization.

Customer satisfaction and loyalty metrics, while often considered external indicators, can reflect internal cultural health. A culture that prioritizes customer-centric values and empowers employees to deliver exceptional service will likely see higher customer satisfaction scores and stronger loyalty. Metrics such as Net Promoter Score (NPS), customer retention rates, and feedback from customer surveys can offer valuable insights into how the internal culture translates into external success.

Leadership effectiveness is another crucial metric, as leaders set the tone for organizational culture. Assessing leadership through 360-degree feedback, leadership development program participation, and succession planning effectiveness can provide an understanding of how well leaders embody and propagate the desired cultural attributes. Strong, culturally aligned leadership is essential for sustaining a culture that supports strategic execution.

By meticulously tracking these key metrics, organizations can gain a comprehensive understanding of their cultural dynamics. This understanding enables leaders to make informed decisions, fostering a culture that not only aligns with but also propels the strategic ambitions of the organization.

Cultural Impact KPI	Measurement Metric
Employee Turnover	**Turnover Percentage**
Time to Market	**Days to Market**
Innovation Rate	**Number of New Ideas Implemented**
Customer Satisfaction	**Net Promoter Score (NPS)**
Employee Engagement	**Employee Engagement Survey Score**

Data Collection and Analysis Techniques

In the realm of business culture, the execution of strategy requires a meticulous approach to understanding the underlying dynamics that drive organizational behavior. To achieve this, a well-structured methodology for data collection and analysis is paramount. The process begins with identifying the key variables that influence business culture, such as leadership styles, communication patterns, employee engagement, and decision-making processes. This identification phase is crucial as it sets the foundation for gathering relevant and actionable data.

Various techniques can be employed to collect data effectively. Surveys and questionnaires are commonly used tools that provide quantitative insights into the attitudes and perceptions of employees. These instruments are designed to capture a broad spectrum of responses, offering a comprehensive view of the organizational climate. They can be administered electronically or in paper form, depending on the accessibility and preferences of the workforce. The questions should be carefully crafted to avoid bias and ensure clarity, thus enabling respondents to provide honest and accurate feedback.

Interviews and focus groups offer a qualitative dimension to data collection, providing deeper insights into the nuances of business culture. Through one-on-one interviews, researchers can explore individual experiences and perspectives, uncovering underlying motivations and sentiments that may not be evident through surveys alone. Focus groups, on the other hand, facilitate dynamic discussions among participants, revealing collective views and shared experiences. These interactive sessions can highlight common themes and divergent opinions, enriching the overall understanding of the organizational environment.

Observational techniques also play a vital role in data collection. By immersing themselves in the daily operations of the organization, researchers can witness firsthand the interactions and behaviors that define the business culture. This method allows for the identification of implicit norms and practices that may not be explicitly articulated by employees. Observations can be conducted overtly or covertly, depending on the context and ethical considerations, but in either case, they provide valuable real-time data that complements other collection methods.

Once the data is collected, the analysis phase begins. Quantitative data from surveys can be analyzed using statistical techniques to identify patterns and correlations. Descriptive statistics, such as mean, median, and standard deviation, offer a snapshot of the central tendencies and variability within the dataset. Inferential statistics, such as regression analysis and hypothesis testing, can be employed to examine relationships between variables and make predictions about future trends. These statistical tools provide a robust framework for interpreting numerical data and drawing evidence-based conclusions.

Qualitative data from interviews and focus groups require a different analytical approach. Content analysis and thematic analysis are commonly used methods to identify recurring themes and patterns within the textual data. By coding the data and categorizing it into meaningful segments, researchers can uncover the underlying narratives that shape the business culture. This process involves a meticulous examination of the text, ensuring that the analysis is both comprehensive and nuanced. The insights gained from qualitative analysis can offer rich contextual understanding, complementing the quantitative findings.

Triangulation is a valuable technique that enhances the reliability and validity of the analysis by combining multiple data sources and methods. By cross-referencing the findings from surveys, interviews, and observations, researchers can corroborate the results and mitigate potential biases. This holistic approach ensures a more accurate and robust interpretation of the business culture, providing a solid foundation for strategy execution.

In essence, the meticulous collection and analysis of data are integral to understanding and shaping business culture. By employing a diverse array of techniques and ensuring rigorous analysis, organizations can gain profound insights into their cultural dynamics, paving the way for effective strategy execution.

Interpreting Cultural Data

Understanding and making sense of cultural data is crucial for executing business strategies effectively. This process involves delving into the subtleties and nuances that define a company's cultural landscape, which can significantly influence the success or failure of strategic initiatives. Cultural data encompasses a wide range of elements, including values, beliefs, customs, rituals, and social behaviors that characterize the workforce and the organization as a whole.

To begin with, gathering cultural data requires a methodical approach. This can be achieved through various means such as surveys, interviews, focus groups, and direct observations. Each method provides unique insights and helps to paint a comprehensive picture of the organizational culture. For instance, surveys can quantify attitudes and perceptions across a large group, while interviews and focus groups allow for deeper exploration of individual and collective experiences.

Once the data is collected, the next step is to analyze it in a way that reveals patterns and trends. This analysis often involves both qualitative and quantitative methods. Quantitative analysis might include statistical techniques to identify correlations and outliers, while qualitative analysis could involve coding and thematic analysis to uncover recurring themes and narratives. It is essential to look beyond the surface-level data and consider the underlying factors that drive certain cultural traits.

An important aspect of interpreting cultural data is understanding the context in which the data was gathered. Cultural elements are often deeply rooted in historical, social, and economic contexts, and these contexts can significantly impact how cultural traits are expressed and perceived. For example, a company with a long history of hierarchical management might exhibit resistance to change, whereas a younger, more dynamic organization might demonstrate a greater openness to innovation.

Moreover, cultural data should be interpreted with an awareness of potential biases. Researchers must be mindful of their own cultural lenses and how these might influence their interpretation of the data. It is beneficial to involve a diverse team in the analysis process to ensure a more balanced and objective perspective. Engaging with different viewpoints can help to mitigate biases and lead to a more accurate understanding of the cultural landscape.

In addition to identifying existing cultural traits, interpreting cultural data also involves recognizing areas for cultural change. This is particularly relevant when aligning culture with strategic goals. For example, if a company's strategy emphasizes customer-centricity but the cultural data reveals a strong internal focus, there may be a need for cultural transformation to support the strategic direction. This requires not only identifying the gap but also understanding the underlying reasons for the current cultural state and developing targeted interventions to bridge the gap.

Effective communication of the findings from cultural data analysis is another critical component. The insights gained need to be translated into actionable recommendations that can be understood and implemented by various stakeholders within the organization. Visual tools such as cultural maps, heat maps, and dashboards can be effective in presenting complex data in an accessible manner.

In conclusion, interpreting cultural data is a multifaceted process that requires a careful and nuanced approach. It involves gathering comprehensive data, analyzing it with both quantitative and qualitative methods, understanding the broader context, being mindful of biases, identifying areas for cultural change, and effectively communicating the findings. By thoroughly interpreting cultural data, organizations can better align their culture with their strategic objectives, ultimately enhancing their ability to execute business strategies successfully.

Case Studies of Measured Impact

In the bustling corridors of global commerce, the interplay between business culture and strategy execution often reveals itself in the most illuminating case studies. These narratives not only showcase the tangible outcomes of aligned organizational efforts but also underscore the nuanced intricacies of cultural dynamics at play. The following cases provide a window into how businesses, through meticulous cultural alignment, have driven remarkable strategic success.

Consider the multinational corporation, TechNova, which undertook a comprehensive cultural overhaul to support its ambitious digital transformation agenda. Facing an industry marked by rapid technological changes and escalating competition, TechNova recognized the imperative of fostering a culture of innovation. By instilling values that encouraged risk-taking and continuous learning, and by implementing cross-functional teams, the company successfully navigated its digital pivot. The impact was profound: a 30% increase in market share within two years, alongside a notable improvement in employee engagement scores. The TechNova case exemplifies how a deliberate cultural shift can facilitate the seamless execution of a strategy that demands agility and forward-thinking.

In another instance, the retail giant ShopEase embarked on a customer-centric strategy to regain its foothold in a saturated market. To align its culture with this strategy, ShopEase introduced a comprehensive training program focused on enhancing customer service skills and fostering a sense of ownership among employees. Additionally, the company restructured its reward system to recognize and celebrate customer-centric behaviors. These cultural adjustments yielded significant dividends. Customer satisfaction scores soared, and the company reported a 15% increase in repeat business within a year. ShopEase's story illustrates the critical role of culture in driving strategic initiatives aimed at enhancing customer loyalty and satisfaction.

Turning to the financial sector, FinServe, a leading banking institution, sought to expand its footprint in the emerging markets. Recognizing the diverse cultural landscapes of these regions, FinServe adopted a localized approach to strategy execution. The company empowered local branches with decision-making authority and encouraged the integration of local cultural nuances into their operations. This decentralization was complemented by a robust framework of shared values and goals that maintained organizational coherence. The results were striking: FinServe's market penetration in emerging economies increased by 25%, and local customer trust levels saw a significant boost. This case underscores the importance of cultural sensitivity and adaptability in executing strategies across diverse geographical landscapes.

A particularly compelling example comes from HealthCore, a healthcare provider that aimed to enhance patient outcomes through a collaborative care model. To support this strategy, the organization cultivated a culture of teamwork and shared responsibility among its staff. Interdisciplinary teams were established, fostering collaboration between doctors, nurses, and administrative personnel. HealthCore also invested in leadership development programs to ensure that managers could effectively nurture this collaborative spirit. The impact was measurable: patient recovery times improved, and the hospital's readmission rates dropped by 20%. HealthCore's experience highlights how fostering a collaborative culture can be instrumental in executing strategies that rely on holistic, integrated approaches.

Lastly, the case of GreenEnergy, a renewable energy firm, offers insights into the role of culture in driving sustainability initiatives. GreenEnergy's strategy centered on innovation and sustainability, underpinned by a culture that valued environmental stewardship and creative problem-solving. The company encouraged employees to propose and pilot green projects, resulting in several successful innovations that reduced operational costs and environmental impact. Over three years, GreenEnergy achieved a 40% reduction in its carbon footprint and saw a corresponding increase in investor confidence. This case illustrates the symbiotic relationship between a culture of innovation and the successful execution of sustainability strategies.

These case studies collectively illuminate the critical interplay between business culture and strategy execution. Each example demonstrates how cultural alignment can propel organizations toward their strategic objectives, yielding measurable impacts that resonate across various dimensions of performance.

Chapter 13

Practical Frameworks for Cultivating Business Culture

Frameworks for Cultural Transformation

Business culture is often the silent force that drives or derails strategy execution. To navigate this complex terrain, organizations need robust frameworks that can guide cultural transformation. These frameworks serve as structured approaches to understanding, diagnosing, and reshaping the cultural elements that influence strategic outcomes.

One foundational framework is the Competing Values Framework (CVF), which categorizes organizational culture into four types: Clan, Adhocracy, Market, and Hierarchy. Each type represents a different set of values and behaviors that can either support or hinder strategy execution. For instance, a Clan culture, which emphasizes collaboration and a family-like atmosphere, may excel in environments where teamwork and employee engagement are critical. On the other hand, a Market culture, focused on competitiveness and achieving tangible results, might be more effective in fast-paced, results-driven industries. By identifying the dominant cultural type within an organization, leaders can tailor their strategies to align with or shift these cultural attributes to better support their strategic goals.

Another pivotal framework is Edgar Schein's model of organizational culture, which delves into the layers of culture: artifacts, espoused values, and underlying assumptions. Artifacts are the visible elements of culture, such as dress codes, office layouts, and formal policies. Espoused values are the stated principles and standards that an organization claims to uphold. Underlying assumptions are the deeply ingrained beliefs and behaviors that are often taken for granted. Understanding these layers helps leaders pinpoint where cultural misalignments may occur and identify the root causes of resistance to change. For example, an organization might espouse innovation as a core value, yet its underlying assumptions may favor risk-averse behaviors, thereby stifling creative initiatives.

The Burke-Litwin Model of Organizational Performance and Change offers another comprehensive approach by linking culture to various organizational dimensions such as leadership, management practices, and external environment. This model emphasizes that cultural change is not an isolated endeavor but is interconnected with other organizational systems. By mapping out these relationships, leaders can develop a holistic strategy that addresses multiple facets of the organization, ensuring that cultural transformation efforts are reinforced by changes in leadership styles, reward systems, and operational processes.

Kotter's 8-Step Change Model provides a sequential approach to cultural transformation, starting from creating a sense of urgency to embedding new approaches within the organizational fabric. This model underscores the importance of building momentum through short-term wins and consolidating gains to ensure lasting change. It highlights that cultural transformation is a process that requires sustained effort and commitment from all levels of the organization.

Lastly, the Denison Organizational Culture Model focuses on four key traits—Mission, Consistency, Involvement, and Adaptability—that are crucial for effective strategy execution. This model posits that a strong mission provides direction and purpose, consistency ensures aligned behaviors, involvement fosters employee engagement, and adaptability enables responsiveness to external changes. By balancing these traits, organizations can create a resilient culture that supports strategic initiatives.

These frameworks provide valuable lenses through which leaders can view and influence their organizational culture. They offer structured methodologies for diagnosing cultural issues, planning interventions, and measuring progress. By leveraging these frameworks, organizations can systematically transform their culture to better align with their strategic objectives, ultimately enhancing their ability to execute strategy and achieve long-term success.

Implementing Cultural Frameworks

A successful strategy execution demands a deep understanding of the cultural dynamics within an organization. Implementing cultural frameworks involves a meticulous process of aligning organizational values, behaviors, and practices with strategic objectives. This alignment is essential for fostering an environment where employees are motivated and equipped to contribute effectively towards the organization's goals.

The first step in implementing cultural frameworks is to conduct a comprehensive cultural assessment. This involves gathering data through surveys, interviews, and observations to understand the existing cultural landscape. Key areas of focus include communication styles, decision-making processes, leadership behaviors, and employee engagement levels. This assessment helps identify cultural strengths and areas that may require change or enhancement.

Once the cultural assessment is complete, it is crucial to define the desired culture that aligns with the strategic objectives. This involves articulating clear values and behaviors that support the organization's vision and mission. Leadership plays a pivotal role in this phase, as they must embody and communicate these values consistently. By setting the tone from the top, leaders can influence the entire organization to adopt the desired cultural traits.

Developing a change management plan is the next critical step. This plan should outline specific actions and initiatives to transition from the current culture to the desired state. Key components of the plan include communication strategies, training programs, and mechanisms for feedback and reinforcement. Effective communication is vital to ensure that all employees understand the rationale behind the cultural change and how it benefits them and the organization.

Training programs are essential to equip employees with the necessary skills and knowledge to adopt new behaviors and practices. These programs should be tailored to address gaps identified during the cultural assessment and align with the strategic objectives. For example, if collaboration is a desired cultural trait, training sessions could focus on teamwork, conflict resolution, and effective communication.

Feedback and reinforcement mechanisms are crucial for sustaining cultural change. Regular feedback loops, such as employee surveys and focus groups, provide valuable insights into the progress of cultural initiatives and highlight areas that may need adjustments. Recognition and reward systems can reinforce desired behaviors and motivate employees to embrace the new culture. Celebrating small wins and acknowledging efforts can create a positive momentum towards achieving the desired cultural state.

It is also important to integrate the cultural framework into organizational processes and systems. This includes aligning performance management systems, recruitment practices, and reward structures with the desired culture. For instance, performance evaluations should assess not only individual achievements but also adherence to cultural values. Recruitment processes should prioritize candidates who demonstrate alignment with the organization's cultural traits.

Monitoring and evaluating the effectiveness of the cultural framework is an ongoing process. Regular assessments and reviews help track progress, identify challenges, and make necessary adjustments. This iterative approach ensures that the cultural framework remains relevant and continues to support the organization's strategic objectives.

In essence, implementing cultural frameworks is a deliberate and systematic process that requires commitment and involvement from all levels of the organization. By aligning cultural traits with strategic goals, organizations can create an environment conducive to successful strategy execution. The key lies in understanding the existing culture, defining the desired state, developing a comprehensive change plan, and continuously monitoring progress to ensure sustained cultural alignment.

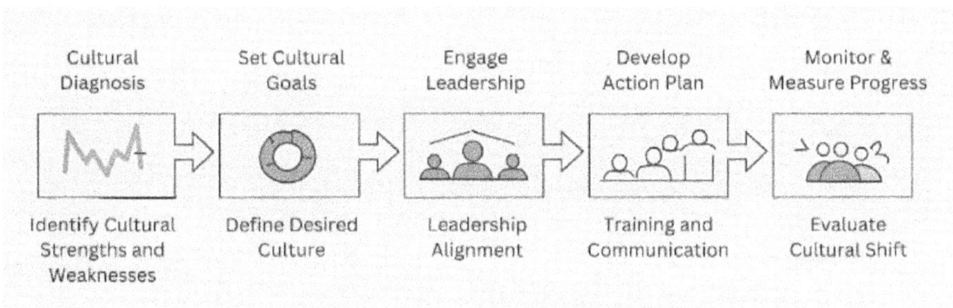

Evaluating Framework Effectiveness

Assessing the effectiveness of a chosen framework within the realm of business culture for strategy execution is pivotal. This process involves a thorough examination of various dimensions to determine how well the framework aligns with organizational goals and cultural attributes.

A key aspect of this evaluation is the alignment between the framework and the company's strategic objectives. A framework that supports and enhances these objectives is more likely to be effective. This requires a deep understanding of both the strategic goals and the cultural nuances of the organization. The framework should not only facilitate the achievement of these goals but also reinforce the cultural values that the organization holds dear.

Another critical factor is the adaptability of the framework. Businesses operate in dynamic environments where change is constant. A framework that can adapt to these changes without losing its core principles is invaluable. This adaptability ensures that the framework remains relevant and effective even as external and internal conditions evolve. It should provide a structure that is flexible enough to accommodate new strategies, technologies, and market conditions.

Employee engagement and buy-in are also crucial for the success of any framework. The attitudes and perceptions of employees towards the framework can significantly impact its effectiveness. If employees perceive the framework as supportive and aligned with their values and work practices, they are more likely to engage with it positively. This engagement can be measured through surveys, feedback sessions, and observing behavioral changes within the organization. High levels of engagement typically indicate that the framework is well-received and is contributing positively to the business culture.

The framework's impact on performance metrics is another important consideration. Quantitative data such as productivity rates, financial performance, and customer satisfaction can provide concrete evidence of the framework's effectiveness. These metrics should be monitored regularly to assess whether the framework is delivering the expected outcomes. Any discrepancies between the expected and actual performance should be analyzed to understand the underlying reasons and make necessary adjustments.

Additionally, the framework should foster communication and collaboration within the organization. Effective strategy execution often requires cross-functional teamwork and transparent communication channels. A framework that promotes these elements can help break down silos and encourage a more cohesive and cooperative work environment. This can lead to more innovative solutions and a stronger alignment between different departments and teams.

The role of leadership in the effectiveness of the framework cannot be overstated. Leaders who actively support and champion the framework can influence its acceptance and implementation across the organization. Their commitment to the framework serves as a model for employees and can drive a cultural shift towards better strategy execution. Leadership buy-in is therefore essential for the framework to gain traction and be integrated into the daily operations of the business.

Regular reviews and updates to the framework are necessary to maintain its effectiveness. As the business landscape changes, so too should the framework. Continuous improvement practices, such as incorporating feedback and learning from past experiences, can help refine the framework. This iterative process ensures that the framework remains a living document that evolves with the organization.

To conclude, evaluating the effectiveness of a framework for strategy execution involves a multifaceted approach. It requires a careful examination of alignment with strategic goals, adaptability, employee engagement, performance metrics, communication, leadership support, and continuous improvement. Each of these elements plays a vital role in determining how well the framework supports the business culture and contributes to successful strategy execution.

Real-World Applications of Cultural Frameworks

In the dynamic landscape of global business, understanding and leveraging cultural frameworks can significantly enhance strategy execution. Cultural frameworks, such as Hofstede's cultural dimensions, Trompenaars' model of national culture differences, and the GLOBE study, offer invaluable insights into the intricate ways culture influences organizational behavior and decision-making.

Consider a multinational corporation aiming to expand its operations into diverse markets. By applying Hofstede's cultural dimensions, the company can tailor its strategies to align with the cultural preferences of the target market. For instance, in high power distance countries, hierarchical organizational structures may be more effective, whereas in low power distance cultures, a more egalitarian approach could foster better employee engagement and productivity.

In the realm of marketing, cultural frameworks can guide the development of campaigns that resonate with local values and norms.

A brand launching a new product in Japan might emphasize harmony and group consensus, reflecting the collectivist nature of Japanese society. Conversely, in individualistic cultures like the United States, marketing strategies might focus on personal achievement and independence, appealing to the cultural ethos of self-reliance.

Human resource management also benefits from the application of cultural frameworks. Trompenaars' model, which includes dimensions such as universalism versus particularism and individualism versus communitarianism, can inform policies on employee relations, conflict resolution, and performance appraisals. In particularist cultures, where relationships and context are paramount, managers might adopt a more flexible approach to rules and policies, whereas in universalist cultures, a consistent and standardized approach would be more appropriate.

The GLOBE study, with its emphasis on leadership behaviors across cultures, provides a comprehensive understanding of how leadership styles need to be adapted to fit cultural expectations. For example, in cultures that score high on the dimension of humane orientation, leaders who demonstrate compassion and support for their employees are likely to be more effective. In contrast, in cultures that value performance orientation, a results-driven leadership style may be more successful.

Real-world applications of cultural frameworks extend to negotiation and conflict resolution. In international negotiations, understanding cultural differences can prevent misunderstandings and foster more productive dialogues. For instance, in cultures with a high context communication style, such as China, negotiators may rely heavily on non-verbal cues and the context surrounding the discussion. In contrast, in low context cultures like Germany, clear and direct communication is preferred.

Furthermore, cultural frameworks can aid in the design of organizational structures and processes that support strategy execution. In cultures with a strong uncertainty avoidance, organizations might implement more detailed planning and control mechanisms to mitigate risks. Conversely, in cultures with low uncertainty avoidance, a more flexible and adaptive approach could be more effective.

By integrating cultural frameworks into strategic planning and execution, businesses can navigate the complexities of global markets with greater agility and precision. These frameworks offer a structured way to understand and respond to cultural differences, enabling organizations to build more cohesive and effective strategies that resonate with diverse stakeholders. Whether expanding into new markets, managing a multicultural workforce, or negotiating international deals, the application of cultural frameworks can provide a significant competitive advantage.

Chapter 14

Future Trends in Business Culture and Strategy Execution

Emerging Trends in Organizational Culture

In the rapidly evolving landscape of business, organizational culture has emerged as a critical component for the successful execution of strategy. Companies are recognizing that a dynamic and adaptive culture can be a significant differentiator in achieving their strategic goals. This shift is driven by several emerging trends that are reshaping how organizations think about and implement their cultural frameworks.

One prominent trend is the increasing emphasis on agility. In an era characterized by rapid technological advancements and market fluctuations, organizations are moving away from rigid, hierarchical structures towards more fluid and flexible models. This shift necessitates a culture that promotes quick decision-making, encourages innovation, and supports continuous learning. Agile cultures prioritize responsiveness and adaptability, enabling organizations to pivot swiftly in response to external changes and internal challenges.

Another significant trend is the focus on inclusivity and diversity. Companies are becoming more aware of the benefits that a diverse workforce brings to the table. A culture that values and leverages diverse perspectives can enhance creativity, improve problem-solving, and drive better decision-making. This trend is not merely about compliance or social responsibility; it is increasingly seen as a strategic imperative that can lead to improved business outcomes. Inclusivity and diversity are being woven into the fabric of organizational culture, influencing hiring practices, team dynamics, and leadership approaches.

The rise of remote work and digital collaboration tools is also transforming organizational culture. The traditional office environment is giving way to virtual workspaces, where geographical boundaries are less relevant. This shift demands a culture that fosters effective communication, trust, and collaboration despite physical distances. Organizations are investing in digital platforms that facilitate seamless interaction and are developing new norms and practices to maintain engagement and cohesion among remote teams.

Employee well-being has gained unprecedented attention as a vital aspect of organizational culture. The recognition that a healthy, satisfied, and motivated workforce is crucial for sustained performance is driving companies to adopt more holistic approaches to employee welfare. This includes not only physical health but also mental and emotional well-being. Organizations are implementing wellness programs, offering flexible work arrangements, and creating supportive environments that help employees balance their professional and personal lives.

Sustainability and corporate social responsibility (CSR) are becoming integral to organizational culture. Stakeholders, including customers, employees, and investors, are increasingly holding companies accountable for their environmental and social impact. A culture that prioritizes sustainability and ethical practices can enhance brand reputation, attract top talent, and build customer loyalty. Companies are integrating sustainable practices into their operations and encouraging employees to contribute to CSR initiatives, thereby embedding these values into their organizational DNA.

Technology is playing a pivotal role in shaping modern organizational cultures. Advanced analytics, artificial intelligence, and machine learning are providing new insights into employee behavior and organizational dynamics. These technologies enable more personalized and data-driven approaches to managing and nurturing culture. For instance, sentiment analysis tools can gauge employee morale, while predictive analytics can identify potential cultural issues before they escalate.

In sum, the evolving trends in organizational culture reflect a broader shift towards more adaptive, inclusive, and responsible business practices. As organizations continue to navigate the complexities of the modern business environment, the ability to cultivate and sustain a positive and forward-thinking culture will be a key determinant of strategic success.

The Future of Work and Its Cultural Implications

The rapid advancement of technology is not just transforming industries but also reshaping the very fabric of work culture. As automation, artificial intelligence, and remote work become more prevalent, organizations are compelled to rethink their strategies for effective execution. The workplace is evolving into a dynamic, interconnected web where flexibility and adaptability are key to sustaining competitive advantage. The traditional nine-to-five office environment is gradually being replaced by more fluid and versatile work arrangements, which necessitate a shift in cultural norms and values.

Remote work, once a perk, has now become a standard practice for many businesses. This shift has profound implications for organizational culture. Physical spaces that once fostered spontaneous interactions and camaraderie are being replaced by virtual environments. The challenge lies in maintaining a cohesive culture where employees feel connected and engaged despite the physical distances. Digital communication tools and platforms play a crucial role in bridging this gap, but they also demand a new set of skills and etiquette to ensure effective collaboration and communication.

The rise of the gig economy further complicates the cultural landscape. With an increasing number of workers opting for freelance or contract-based roles, the concept of job security and loyalty is undergoing a transformation. Organizations must find innovative ways to integrate these transient workers into their cultural framework, ensuring they feel valued and aligned with the company's mission and values. This requires a more inclusive and flexible approach to culture-building, one that accommodates diverse working styles and preferences.

Artificial intelligence and automation are not just changing the nature of tasks but also the skills required to perform them. As routine jobs become automated, there is a growing emphasis on creativity, critical thinking, and emotional intelligence. These skills are inherently human and cannot be replicated by machines. Consequently, organizational culture must evolve to nurture these attributes, fostering an environment that encourages continuous learning and innovation. This cultural shift is essential for organizations to remain agile and responsive in a rapidly changing business landscape.

The future of work also brings to the forefront issues of diversity and inclusion. As workforces become more global and diverse, organizations must strive to create cultures that celebrate differences and promote equity. This involves not only addressing visible aspects of diversity such as race and gender but also embracing a broader spectrum that includes diverse perspectives, experiences, and ideas. A culture that values diversity and inclusion is more likely to drive innovation and better decision-making, ultimately contributing to more effective strategy execution.

Sustainability and corporate social responsibility are becoming integral to business strategy, reflecting a shift in cultural values towards more ethical and responsible practices. Employees, especially younger generations, are increasingly seeking purpose and meaning in their work. They want to be part of organizations that contribute positively to society and the environment. This necessitates a cultural alignment where business goals are harmonized with broader societal values, ensuring that strategy execution is not only profitable but also sustainable and ethical.

In this evolving landscape, leadership plays a critical role in shaping and sustaining an adaptive and resilient culture. Leaders must be visionaries who can navigate through uncertainty and inspire their teams to embrace change. They must cultivate trust, transparency, and a sense of shared purpose, creating an environment where employees are motivated to contribute their best towards the organization's strategic objectives.

As the future of work continues to unfold, the cultural implications are profound and far-reaching. Organizations that proactively adapt their cultures to align with these emerging trends will be better positioned to execute their strategies effectively and thrive in the new world of work.

Adapting to Future Cultural Shifts

In the ever-evolving landscape of global commerce, the ability to anticipate and adapt to cultural shifts is paramount for organizations striving to execute their strategies effectively. Business culture, a complex tapestry woven from the threads of shared values, beliefs, and practices, does not exist in a vacuum. It is constantly influenced by external trends, demographic changes, technological advancements, and socio-political movements. Leaders who recognize this dynamic nature and prepare their organizations for impending cultural shifts stand a better chance of maintaining relevance and achieving long-term success.

To begin with, understanding the trajectory of cultural trends requires a keen eye and a proactive mindset. Organizations must invest in continuous learning and development programs that not only educate employees about current cultural dynamics but also equip them with the tools to anticipate future changes. This involves fostering a culture of curiosity and openness, where employees are encouraged to explore diverse perspectives and challenge the status quo. By cultivating such an environment, businesses can remain agile and responsive to shifts that may impact their strategic objectives.

Moreover, leveraging data analytics and cultural intelligence can provide valuable insights into emerging trends. Advanced data analytics tools can identify patterns and predict potential cultural changes by analyzing vast amounts of information from various sources, including social media, market research, and consumer behavior studies. By integrating these insights into their strategic planning processes, organizations can better align their business practices with the evolving cultural landscape.

Another critical aspect of adapting to future cultural shifts is the role of leadership. Leaders must exemplify cultural adaptability and demonstrate a commitment to inclusivity and diversity. This involves not only setting the tone from the top but also ensuring that these values permeate every level of the organization. By fostering an inclusive culture, businesses can harness the diverse perspectives and experiences of their employees, which can lead to more innovative solutions and better decision-making.

Furthermore, organizations should establish mechanisms for continuous feedback and dialogue. Creating platforms where employees can voice their opinions and share their experiences fosters a sense of belonging and helps identify potential cultural shifts early on. Regularly conducting cultural audits and employee surveys can provide insights into the prevailing cultural climate within the organization and highlight areas that may require attention or adjustment.

Adapting to cultural shifts also necessitates a flexible approach to policies and practices. Organizations must be willing to reassess and modify their existing frameworks to align with changing cultural norms and expectations. This could involve revisiting policies related to work-life balance, remote work, diversity and inclusion, and employee well-being. By staying attuned to the evolving needs and preferences of their workforce, businesses can create a more supportive and engaging environment that drives performance and retention.

Lastly, collaboration and partnership with external stakeholders can enhance an organization's ability to navigate cultural shifts. Engaging with industry peers, academic institutions, and cultural experts can provide fresh perspectives and innovative ideas. Participation in industry forums and cultural exchange programs can also facilitate the sharing of best practices and foster a deeper understanding of global cultural trends.

In essence, the capacity to adapt to future cultural shifts is not merely a reactive endeavor but a strategic imperative. Organizations that prioritize cultural adaptability and embed it into their core operations can better navigate the complexities of the global business environment and execute their strategies with greater efficacy. By doing so, they not only safeguard their competitive edge but also contribute to a more inclusive and dynamic business landscape.

Predictions for Strategy Execution in Future Cultures

The landscape of strategy execution is on the cusp of transformative evolution, driven by rapid technological advancements, shifting socio-economic dynamics, and an increasingly interconnected global marketplace. Future cultures will demand a more nuanced approach to strategy, one that is adaptable, inclusive, and deeply integrated with the digital fabric of modern business.

Organizations will need to cultivate a culture that is agile and resilient. The traditional hierarchical structures will give way to more fluid and decentralized models. These models will empower employees at all levels to make decisions and take initiative, fostering a sense of ownership and accountability. As a result, businesses will be able to respond swiftly to market changes and emerging opportunities, maintaining a competitive edge in a fast-paced environment.

Digital transformation will play a pivotal role in shaping future business cultures. The integration of artificial intelligence, machine learning, and big data analytics will revolutionize how strategies are formulated and executed. Predictive analytics will enable businesses to anticipate trends and customer needs with unprecedented accuracy, allowing for more informed and proactive decision-making. This technological integration will also necessitate a culture of continuous learning and innovation, as employees will need to stay abreast of the latest tools and methodologies to remain effective.

In future cultures, diversity and inclusion will be paramount. A diverse workforce brings a wealth of perspectives and ideas, driving creativity and innovation. Inclusive cultures will not only attract top talent from various backgrounds but also foster a collaborative environment where all voices are heard and valued. This will be crucial for strategy execution, as diverse teams are better equipped to identify potential challenges and devise comprehensive solutions.

Sustainability will become a core component of business strategy. As environmental concerns continue to rise, companies will be expected to integrate sustainable practices into their operations. This shift will require a cultural commitment to sustainability, where every decision is made with consideration for its environmental impact. Businesses that prioritize sustainability will not only benefit from a positive public image but also from long-term cost savings and operational efficiencies.

The future workplace will be increasingly remote and flexible, further influencing strategy execution. With the rise of remote work, companies will need to build a culture of trust and accountability, where employees are empowered to manage their own time and deliver results without constant supervision. Effective communication and collaboration tools will be essential to maintain cohesion and ensure that strategic objectives are met.

Leadership will also evolve to meet the demands of future cultures. Leaders will need to be more empathetic, adaptive, and visionary. They will play a crucial role in fostering a positive culture, guiding their teams through change, and ensuring that the organization's strategic goals are aligned with its cultural values. Leadership development programs will need to focus on these new competencies to prepare future leaders for the challenges ahead.

Future business cultures will be characterized by a blend of technological prowess, human-centric values, and a commitment to sustainability. Organizations that can effectively integrate these elements into their strategy execution will be well-positioned to thrive in the ever-changing global marketplace. The ability to adapt, innovate, and lead with empathy will be the defining traits of successful businesses in the years to come.

Reference List and Bibliography

Books

1. **Kotter, J. P.** (1996). *Leading Change*. Harvard Business Review Press.
    - A seminal work on change management and the importance of aligning organizational culture with strategic change.
2. **Schein, E. H.** (2010). *Organizational Culture and Leadership*. Jossey-Bass.
    - Provides an in-depth analysis of how organizational culture influences leadership and strategic outcomes.
3. **Collins, J.** (2001). *Good to Great: Why Some Companies Make the Leap... and Others Don't*. HarperBusiness.
    - Explores the role of culture in transforming organizations from good to great.
4. **Barney, J. B.** (1986). *Organizational Culture: Can It Be a Source of Competitive Advantage?*. Academy of Management Review, 11(3), 656-665.
    - An influential paper discussing how organizational culture can provide a competitive edge.
5. **Cameron, K. S., & Quinn, R. E.** (2011). *Diagnosing and Changing Organizational Culture: Based on the Competing Values Framework*. Jossey-Bass.
    - Offers tools and methodologies for assessing and changing organizational culture to align with strategic goals.

6. **Denison, D. R.** (1990). *Corporate Culture and Organizational Effectiveness*. Wiley.

    - Analyzes how corporate culture impacts organizational effectiveness and strategy execution.

Research Papers

1. **Hofstede, G., Hofstede, G. J., & Minkov, M.** (2010). *Cultures and Organizations: Software of the Mind*. McGraw-Hill.

    - A comprehensive study on how cultural differences impact organizational practices and strategic execution.

2. **Kotter, J. P., & Heskett, J. L.** (1992). *Corporate Culture and Performance*. Free Press.

    - Examines the relationship between corporate culture and business performance, providing empirical evidence.

3. **Edgar Schein, E.** (1996). *Three Cultures of Management: The Key to Organizational Learning*. MIT Sloan Management Review.

    - Discusses the impact of different types of management cultures on organizational learning and strategy.

4. **Peters, T. J., & Waterman, R. H.** (1982). *In Search of Excellence: Lessons from America's Best-Run Companies*. Harper & Row.

    - Highlights the role of cultural values in the success of leading companies.

5. **Gordon, G. G., & DiTomaso, N.** (1992). *Predicting Corporate Performance from Organizational Culture*. Journal of Management Studies, 29(6), 783-798.

    - Investigates how different cultural attributes can predict organizational performance.

Articles

1. **"How Culture Drives Strategy Execution"** (2020). *Harvard Business Review*.
    - Discusses the importance of aligning organizational culture with strategic execution.
2. **"The Role of Culture in Strategy Implementation"** (2019). *Journal of Business Strategy*.
    - Analyzes case studies and research on how culture impacts the implementation of business strategies.
3. **"Aligning Organizational Culture with Business Strategy"** (2018). *MIT Sloan Management Review*.
    - Explores practical approaches for aligning culture with business strategy.
4. **"The Intersection of Culture and Strategy"** (2021). *Forbes Magazine*.
    - Provides insights into how successful companies manage the intersection between culture and strategy.

Websites

1. **Harvard Business Review (HBR)**. www.hbr.org
    - Offers numerous articles and case studies on culture and strategy alignment.
2. **MIT Sloan Management Review**. sloanreview.mit.edu
    - Features research and articles on the role of culture in business strategy.

3. **McKinsey & Company**. www.mckinsey.com
   - Provides reports and insights on organizational culture and strategy execution.
4. **Gallup**. www.gallup.com
   - Offers research and data on employee engagement and organizational culture.
5. **Deloitte Insights**. www2.deloitte.com
   - Features articles and reports on the impact of culture on business strategy

www.ingramcontent.com/pod-product-compliance
Lightning Source LLC
LaVergne TN
LVHW021139160826
845679LV00023B/1966